THE
HALLWAY
TRILOGY

THE
HALLWAY
TRILOGY

Includes

ROSE
PARAFFIN
NURSING

By Adam Rapp

THEATRE COMMUNICATIONS GROUP
NEW YORK
2013

The Hallway Trilogy is published by Theatre Communications Group, Inc., 520 Eighth Avenue, 24th Floor, New York, NY 10018-4156

The publication of *The Hallway Trilogy*, by Adam Rapp, through TCG's Book Program, is made possible in part by the New York State Council on the Arts with the support of Governor Andrew Cuomo and the New York State Legislature.

TCG books are exclusively distributed to the book trade by Consortium Book Sales and Distribution.

LIBRARY OF CONGRESS CATALOGING-IN-PUBLICATION DATA
Rapp, Adam.
The Hallway trilogy : Includes Rose, Paraffin, Nursing / Adam Rapp.
—First Edition.
pages cm
ISBN 978-1-55936-416-4 (pbk.)
ISBN 978-1-55936-432-4 (ebook)
I. Title.
PS3568.A6278H35 2014
813'.54—dc23
2013030568

Book design and composition by Lisa Govan
Cover design by Mark Melnick
Front cover photo by Glenn Fitzgerald
Back cover photo courtesy of the author
First Edition, December 2013

For Katherine Waterston

CONTENTS

THE
HALLWAY
TRILOGY

Production History

The Hallway Trilogy received its world premiere at Rattlestick Playwrights Theater (David Van Asselt, Artistic Director; Brian Long, Managing Director) on February 25, 2011. Part One, *Rose*, was directed by Adam Rapp; Part Two, *Paraffin*, was directed by Daniel Aukin; and Part Three, *Nursing*, was directed by Trip Cullman. The set design was by Beowulf Boritt, the costume design was by Jessica Pabst, the lighting design was by Tyler Micoleau, the sound design and music were by Eric Shimelonis; the production stage managers were Melissa Mae Gregus and Meredith Dixon. The cast included:

OREST FEDATOV/DENNY KELLEN	William Apps
IDO LEVY/JOE BOYD	Robert Beitzel
EUGENE "JACK" O'NEILL/MARTY KUBIAK	Guy Boyd
JERRY WALSH/ANDY	Louis Cancelmi
RAHEL LEVY/JOAN	Maria Dizzia
RICHARD BUMPER/LLOYD BOYD	Logan Marshall-Green
DENA PASZEK/TOUR GUIDE	Sue Jean Kim
MARBLES/LESHIK	Nick Lawson
MEGAN RIDGLEY/ERIN	Sarah Lemp
LOUIE ZAPPALEO/KEVIN O'NEILL	Danny Mastrogiorgio
MARY SAOGRAOBH/MARGO KELLEN	Julianne Nicholson
LUCAS KELLEN/JOURNALIST	Jeremy Strong
ROSE HATHAWAY	Katherine Waterston
CORY/GUARD	Stephen Tyrone Williams

ROSE

CHARACTERS

MARY SAOGRAOBH (pronounced "Seagrave"), pretty, thirty-two

EUGENE "JACK" O'NEILL, superintendent, mid-sixties

MARBLES, twenty-five

ROSE HATHAWAY, mid-twenties

OREST FEDATOV, Russian immigrant, thirties

JERRY WALSH, late twenties

MEGAN RIDGLEY, Mary's sister, late twenties

LOUIE ZAPPALEO, Italian, forties

RICHARD BUMPER, Rose's husband, late twenties

SETTING

A third-floor hallway of a pre-war tenement apartment building on the Lower East Side of Manhattan, 1953.

The third-story hallway of a pre-war tenement apartment build-ing on the Lower East Side of Manhattan, Saturday, November 28th, 1953. The original floorboards are covered with one-foot-square tiles of speckled linoleum. Pale green walls, a sconce lamp with a broken bulb. There are four units: Unit Seven extreme stage right, and then moving stage left, Unit Eight, Unit Nine and Unit Ten. The stairwell is just stage right of Unit Seven. There are two undressed windows overlooking a courtyard, one half open, a fire escape slanting across their panes. Between Units Seven and Eight, is a Model 50, early-1950s-style ten-cent pay phone, a standing ashtray beside it.

On the wall between Unit Seven and the pay phone, someone has painted in black: MICKEY MOUSE IS WATCHING.

In front of condemned Unit Eight, pushed up against the wall and blocking its door, is an old upright piano, closed. It has a proper piano bench with a convertible top. Downstage of Unit Ten's door stands an old, cold radiator.

Unit Seven's door is ajar. A radio can be heard coming from inside.

It is early evening, just before dinnertime. There is a hint of rain in the air and the light in an upstage window should suggest cloud cover.

Moments later, a woman ascends the stairwell. She is well-dressed in a nice coat, nylons and a nice pair of shoes. She carries a nice purse. She is tired, dejected, bordering on total anguish. She makes her way up the stairs. She stops to read the painted message on the wall, continues up the stairs.

Moments later we hear her attempting to key into her apartment, then, "Damnit to hell!"

This same woman, Mary Saograobh (pronounced "Seagrave"), enters from the stairwell. She is thirty-two, pretty, a redhead, a hint of cunning in her eyes. She has shed her coat, but still holds her purse. She wears a nice blouse and a skirt, lipstick with matching nail polish. She crosses to Unit Ten, presses her ear to the door, listens. She takes out a compact, opens it, checks her reflection, takes in her fatigue, powders her face, closes the compact, puts it away. She knocks, waits. No answer.

Unit Seven's door closes, the sound of the radio is muffled now. Mary knocks again.

O'NEILL *(Off)*: Who is it?

MARY: Mr. O'Neill, it's Mary Saograobh from Apartment Twelve.

O'NEILL *(Off)*: Whattaya want?

MARY: I'm sorry to disturb you, Mr. O'Neill, but it appears that my key isn't working properly. Did you change the locks again?

O'NEILL *(Off)*: Did I what?

MARY *(Louder)*: I asked if you changed the locks again.

O'NEILL *(Off)*: Maybe I did, maybe I didn't.

MARY: Mr. O'Neill, there's really no need to be coy.

O'NEILL *(Off)*: I told your sister a thousand times: You don't pay your rent on time, I change the locks! It's a simple procedure! First of the month. You've had damn near four weeks!

MARY: I realize that, Mr. O'Neill, but last week my sister did give you twenty dollars as a guarantee.

o'neill *(Off)*: Guaranteeing what, friendship?! Oxygen?! A measly twenty bucks? This isn't a goddamn flophouse!

mary: Could you at least open the door so we can discuss this civilly.

o'neill *(Off)*: So we can do what?

mary: Discuss this civilly.

o'neill *(Off)*: You tryin' to suggest I'm somethin' I'm not?

mary: I'm not trying to suggest anything, Mr. O'Neill. I simply asked if we could lose the door and speak civilly with each other.

(Mary produces a cigarette from a gold case. The pay phone rings. Mary lights the cigarette, smokes.)

o'neill *(Off)*: Aren't you gonna answer that?

mary: I wasn't expecting a call.

o'neill *(Off)*: It's common courtesy to answer a ringing phone.

(Mary crosses to the phone, answers it, still smoking.)

mary *(Into phone)*: Hello . . . Whom may I say is calling? . . . One moment, please.

(She sets the receiver down, crosses to Mr. O'Neill's door.)

Mr. O'Neill, are you still there?

o'neill *(Off)*: Well, I didn't die, if that's what you're wonderin'.

mary: There's a man on the phone for you.

o'neill *(Off)*: Who is it?

mary: He said his name is Louie Zap.

o'neill *(Off)*: Tell him I'm out.

mary: He says he's quite certain that you're on the premises.

o'neill *(Off)*: Tell him I died.

mary: Really?

o'neill *(Off)*: Yeah, tell him I died and went to Heaven.

(Mary crosses back to the phone.)

MARY *(Into phone)*: Mr. Zap, it appears that Mr. O'Neill is dead . . .
Yes, that's correct, he died and went to Heaven . . . I don't
know . . . Uh-huh . . . No, I'm not his secretary—I live in
his building . . . Well, whomever's building then . . . Okay,
I'll give him the message.

*(She hangs up, checks the coin slot, removes a red Super
Ball, puts it in her pocket, returns to O'Neill's door, her back
against it now, resting.)*

He says he'll be coming by later. And wishes you a safe
return from your, um, Heavenly excursion . . . Mr. O'Neill?

O'NEILL *(Off)*: I heardya. Go away.

MARY: Will you please open the door? I have something for you.

O'NEILL *(Off)*: What.

MARY: Well, it's a surprise.

O'NEILL *(Off)*: If it's not the eighty-five dollars your sister owes
me, I'm not interested.

MARY: Unfortunately it's not the balance of the rent. But it's such
a pleasant surprise . . . Would you care for some company?

O'NEILL *(Off)*: Company! I already got company!

MARY: I wasn't aware—

O'NEILL *(Off)*: I always got company. People comin' around. People needin' things. I'm not that old.

MARY: No one said anything about you being old.

O'NEILL *(Off)*: I've done a lotta things in this lifetime. Spent my
youth on coal barges. Damn near lost my leg. Damn near
lost everything I had . . . I got nothing but company. I got
a cat.

(Mary sits on the cold radiator, checks her stocking.)

MARY: I thought pets weren't allowed in this building.

O'NEILL *(Off)*: They are in *my* unit.

MARY: Well, you are the superintendent.

O'NEILL *(Off)*: You're damn right about that.

MARY: . . . What's his name?

O'NEILL *(Off)*: Who?

MARY: Your cat.

O'NEILL *(Off)*: . . . Julius.

MARY: Julius. I'll bet he's just the cutest little thing. *(Calling through the door)* Hi, Julius. Here, kitty, kitty.

O'NEILL *(Off)*: He's not little. And he's not cute, either. He's got the face of a walleyed Negro. Mustafa the Walleyed Negro. Thinks he's all-important.

(Mary stands, fighting fatigue, moves back to the door.)

MARY: Well, perhaps you and Julius—or Mustafa the, um . . .

O'NEILL *(Off)*: Walleyed Negro.

MARY: Yes, perhaps you and your kitty cat would enjoy a little company? Like I said, I have a surprise for you.

O'NEILL *(Off)*: Is it a ham?

MARY: A ham? No, Mr. O'Neill, it's not a ham.

O'NEILL: That's about the only thing I like anymore: ham. And maybe some corn.

(A man called Marbles ascends the stairwell. He is perhaps twenty-five, wears a large tweed overcoat, a Mao Communist cap, baggy pants, a colorful scarf and old black shoes. He carries a live pigeon under his arm, a carrier note attached to its leg. He releases the pigeon through the window.)

MARY: Why don't you be a sport and open the door?

O'NEILL *(Off)*: If this is a trick I'm kickin' you outta the building, plain and simple. You and your sister, the schoolteacher. What's her name again?

MARY: Megan.

O'NEILL *(Off)*: Yeah, Megan. Since when can't a schoolteacher come up with a hundred and five dollars for rent?

MARY: Unfortunately public schoolteachers don't earn a very good living.

(Marbles approaches Mary with a lightbulb, changes out the dead bulb in the sconce lamp, then holds out his hand. Mary produces the red Super Ball she acquired from the pay phone, hands it to him. He bounces it on the floor, catches it in his cap. Then he goes to his knees, begs her for her cigarette. She gives it to him. He takes it, crosses to the stairwell.)

O'NEILL *(Off)*: Save it for the mayor's office . . . What kind of a last name is Sauerkraut anyway?

MARY: It's pronounced "Seagrave" and it's Irish.

O'NEILL *(Off)*: It don't look like "Seagrave" on your mailbox. Looks like sauerkraut.

MARY: That's the Gaelic spelling.

O'NEILL *(Off)*: Goddamn Gaelics. Shoulda known better. Gaelics and Eye-talians are taking over the whole neighborhood.

MARY: I'm sorry you feel that way.

O'NEILL *(Off)*: Oh, don't waste your sorrow on me! Save it for the ones who need it! The harlots and the hobos. And that blind bastard with the Jesus sign over on Delancey. Mr. Nail-me-to-the-cross-of-shame. Milky-eyed blind bastard.

(From his pocket, Marbles produces an old bottle of rye, hides it behind the water pipe next to Unit Seven's door, then caws like a crow and disappears down the stairwell.)

(Off) Is there a goddamn crow out there?

MARY: It's just me . . . Mr. O'Neill, don't you want to see your surprise?

O'NEILL *(Off)*: Any shenanigans and you can consider yourself evicted.

(The door opens partway, still held by the chain, O'Neill's face in the opening. Then he releases the chain and Eugene "Jack" O'Neill stands before Mary. He is a large man in his mid-sixties. He wears boxer shorts, an old wife-beater, black socks, slippers and some sort of robe. He stands using a cane.

*He looks haggard, angry. He's very much alone in the world.
He's probably drunk.)*

MARY *(Fun)*: Hiya.

(O'Neill grunts.)

Whattaya doing in there?

O'NEILL: What am I doin'?

MARY: Yeah, you keeping yourself busy?

O'NEILL: I'm not doin' nothin'. Why, what the hell are *you* doin'?

MARY: I'm standing here talking to you. Nice slippers, by the by.

*(He looks down at his slippers, then quickly turns back toward
his unit.)*

O'NEILL: Julius, get down offa there! I toldya a thousand times . . .
Goddamn cat. *(Turning back, suddenly recognizing her)*
Hey, you're that girl.

MARY: What girl?

O'NEILL: The one from the newspapers. The one who was s'posed
to marry that fat sonuvabitch from East Hampton. Whosi-
whatsit. Jackie Jingleheimer or whatever his name is. That
tubbalard in the tuxedo.

MARY: His name is Joshua Jorgensen.

O'NEILL: Yeah, old candy-ass Jim Jorgensen with the French
sports car and the sunburn.

*(He starts down the hallway, looking for something, opens
the lid of the piano bench, closes it, continues on toward the
stairwell.)*

(Searching) Rich guys who are that fat don't deserve to be
tan. And how the hell does he even get in that little car of
his, anyway? With a goddamn *winch*? Stick a harpoon in
'em, that's what I say.

MARY: Nothing would make me happier, actually.

(O'Neill continues his search near the stairwell, no luck.)

O'NEILL: And what's with that hair? Looks like a goddamn potato pancake on his head. A potato pancake with owl feathers. *(Closing the window)* Talk about offensive. He's old enough to be your father. How old are you anyway?

MARY *(Lying)*: I'm twenty-seven, why?

O'NEILL: Twenty-seven . . . Old Jingleheimer must be twice your age.

(O'Neill discovers the bottle of rye wedged between the corner and the water pipe. He reaches down, grabs it, puts it in the pocket of his robe.)

Weren't you supposed to marry that enormous sonuvabitch?

MARY: We were to be married, yes.

O'NEILL: Yeah, what the hell happened there?

MARY: Sometimes things just don't work out.

O'NEILL *(Approaching Mary)*: What happened is you got caught with that young fella out in Sag Harbor. That's what it said in the goddamn *Daily News*, at least. I got it right in there. *(Exiting briefly to get the newspaper, then returning)* That Mexican kid with the sailboat.

MARY: He's not Mexican, he's from Spain. And it wasn't a sailboat, it was a yacht.

O'NEILL: Yeah, Georgie Picante, the Mexican Spaniard in the bikini underthings.

MARY: Peroni. Jorge Peroni. And that was a swimsuit. A legitimate swimsuit.

O'NEILL: Maybe by European standards. Boy, they certainly caught you two red-handed. Couldn't help yourself, couldya? You really blew that one. *(Offering the newspaper and a pen)* Here, sign this for me. Right there on the leg. To Gene . . .

(She stands there, humiliated, then takes the pen, signs the newspaper, returns it.)

So what's the big surprise?

MARY *(Still thrown by the newspaper)*: Surprise?

O'NEILL: You been standin' here for godknowshowlong, promisin' some big surprise . . . You got a salami sandwich in your purse or somethin'?

MARY: The surprise is me.

O'NEILL: You? What the hell's so surprisin' about you?

(She opens her blouse, stands before him. He stares at her, mesmerized.)

MARY: May I come in, Mr. O'Neill?

(He looks down the hallway, makes sure the coast is clear, steps aside, lets her in, closes and chains the door.

Moments later, a young woman enters from the stairwell. She is mid-twenties, tall, thin, beautiful, somehow lost. She wears a nice dress and her face is made up, her hair tastefully done. She wears a nice coat, maybe something with a little fur. She carries a purse, gloves. She looks almost as if she has prepared for a very important audition and has finally made her way to the correct bungalow on the studio lot. She often fidgets nervously, but it may manifest only in her trembling hands. She walks slowly down the hall, toward Mr. O'Neill's door, Unit Ten, approaches it as if in a dream. She stops, several feet away from his door, gathers her will.

From the stairwell, a single marble is launched and rolls slowly toward her. She turns, bends down, picks it up, but no one is there. She places the marble in her purse.

She turns back to the door, approaches it, knocks, waits, nothing. She knocks again. Nothing. She places her ear to the door, listens. The pay phone rings, startling her. It rings five times, ceases.

She touches the cold radiator, sits on it.

The sound of a horn can be heard being played from inside Unit Seven. Rose turns to the sound, listens. It is a plaintive, beautiful sound. She crosses to Unit Seven, knocks on the door. The sound of the horn ceases. The door opens. Orest Fedatov, a Russian immigrant in his early thirties, stands in the doorway, holding a brass horn. He wears a long thermal white T-shirt, with another shirt over it, and simple trousers. He is barefoot.)

 OREST: Yes?

ROSE: I'm terribly sorry for disturbing you, but I was wondering if you could tell me if Mr. O'Neill lives here.

OREST: Mr. O'Neill live down the hall. In Apartment Ten.

ROSE: Yes, I thought so, thank you. Do you have any idea if he's home?

OREST: I do not have any idea. He is sometimes there and he is sometimes not there. He is building—how you say—leader.

ROSE: Oh, he's the super?

OREST: He is super, yes.

ROSE: Mr. O'Neill's the super. Well, that's . . . that's very interesting. How clever.

OREST: I would advice you to knock on his door.

ROSE: I did that already. There was no answer.

OREST: Perhaps he is in toilet.

ROSE: Perhaps he is.

OREST: Perhaps he is in toilet or perhaps he is overtaking himself in tub of the shower.

ROSE: If that's the case I'll try again in a few minutes . . . By the way, was that you playing the trumpet?

OREST: It is cornet. They are not same device, but very close. Many people confuse themselves.

ROSE: You play so beautifully.

OREST: I play like, how you say . . . horse with backside on the shoulders.

ROSE: Oh, that's not true.

OREST: My tone is coarse like side of building.

ROSE: I thought what I heard was lovely.

OREST: I have the lip of pigeon. It is weak. I hope to some day play like Louis Armstrong. Do you know this fantastic human person?

ROSE: Of course. Louis Armstrong is quite famous.

OREST: "Potato Head Blues" and "Muggles" are perhaps greatest jazz compositions in world history.

ROSE: Do you play professionally?

OREST: Two times. I play jazz festival in St. Louis, Mississippi—

ROSE: Missouri.

OREST: I mean St. Louis, Missouri. And I substitute in New Haven Symphony Orchestra for one week and two days. I have audition for to play opera at City Center.

ROSE: That's very exciting. When is your audition?

OREST: On Tuesday of week forthcoming.

ROSE: Which opera is it?

OREST: It is called *Lohengrin* by superlative German composer, Richard Wagner.

ROSE: I think opera is so beautiful. The Italian operas especially. Puccini's *Madame Butterfly* might be my favorite. I wish you luck on your audition.

OREST: Thank you.

ROSE: You're welcome. My name is Rose by the way. Rose Hathaway.

(She holds her hand out. They shake.)

OREST: Hello, Rose . . . Ha . . .

ROSE: . . . Hathaway.

OREST: Rose Hathaway . . .

ROSE: Yes.

OREST: Hello, Rose Hathaway. Good afternoon.

(He kisses her hand.)

ROSE: Hello.

OREST: Hello, yes.

ROSE: And what is your name?

OREST: Orest Maksimovich Fedatov.

ROSE: Orest Mak . . .

OREST: . . . simovich.

ROSE: Maksimovich.

OREST: Fedatov.

ROSE: Orest Maksimovich Fedatov.

OREST: Yes.

ROSE: Hello, Orest Maksimovich Fedatov.

OREST: Hello, Rose Hathaway. Good afternoon.

(He kisses her hand again.)

ROSE: Good afternoon. *(Breaking the handshake finally)* Orest Maksimovich Fedatov. Wow. Saying your name puts the most interesting feeling in my mouth. It's like eating lobster on Cape Cod.

OREST: I have no idea what this means.

ROSE: It doesn't matter. It's very nice to meet you, Orest.

OREST: It's very nice to meet you in equal measurements. I am filled with explosive apologies for destruction to your name.

ROSE: Oh, heavens, don't worry about it, Orest. You have a wonderful accent by the way. Where are you from?

OREST: I am from Russia. But I love America so much. I would do anything to stay here. I would fight in war. I would kill millions of people. I would stab millions and millions of people to stay in America. Or attack them with giant sword with red, white and blue flag tied around my legs and buttocks.

(He notices the painted words on the wall next to his door.)

Mickey Mouse is watching. Stupid Mouse.

ROSE: Are you from Moscow? The only reason I ask is because I understand there are exceptional theater artists from Moscow. I'm an actress, so I've read a lot about a technique created by the great Konstantin Stanislavsky at the Moscow Arts Theatre and all of his work with Anton Chekhov.

OREST: I am not from Moscow. I am from Taganrog. A metropolis on Sea of Azov.

ROSE: Oh, the Sea of Azov. That sounds so mysterious.

OREST: It is also known as the most shallow sea on the earth. You could not even lose a kopek in this sea.

ROSE: I didn't know that.

OREST: I think Moscow is disgusting Communist sewer filled with liars and skinny whores possessing syphilis. America is far superior place.

ROSE: I'm so glad you like it here.

OREST: Chekhov were from my hometown.

ROSE: The great Anton Chekhov? How wonderful.

OREST: There are many statues.

ROSE: I can only imagine.

OREST: To me his plays are so boring they make my brains to harden like field of cow shit. Louis Armstrong is far superior man. He is American legend, and I love his thick black skin. I would like to some day become black American jazz Jesus . . . I mean genius.

(Suddenly, the sound of a woman moaning in Russian from the back of Orest's apartment. It is the kind of anguish that speaks to undeniable human suffering.)

(To his mother, in Russian) A lady in the hallway.

(More moaning.)

(To his mother, in Russian) I'm coming, I'm coming . . . *(To Rose, in English)* If you will excuse me please. My mother . . . she is very sick and fat.

(He closes the door in her face. Rose is left standing there alone.)

ROSE: Nice to meet you.

(Some heated Russian discussion between Orest and his mother. Maybe a broken dish. Moments later, the horn starts to play again, despite the complaints coming from Orest's mother.

Rose turns and faces Mr. O'Neill's door again, then pulls out the piano bench, sits.

Marbles enters from the stairwell. He is holding a shoe box. He crosses to Rose with the shoe box, sets it on top of the piano, sits next to her, lifts the lid on the piano, starts to play along to the trumpet. He is silly and flirtatious. At first his piano playing is slow and mournful, in rhythm with the trumpet, then it breaks the time signature and evolves into a full-out boogie-woogie arrangement. Then he stands, starts snapping his fingers, produces a harmonica, dances and plays the blues.

The trumpet stops. Unit Seven's door flies open. Orest stands there, angry. Marbles ceases playing.)

OREST: You ruin the world with your boogie-woogie! Please stop ruining world! *(To Rose)* Hello, Rose Hathaway. Good afternoon.

ROSE: Good afternoon, Orest.

OREST *(To Marbles)*: If you think you are smart, Mr. Marbles, you have shit for brains. *(To Rose)* If you will excuse me, thank you.

(Orest goes back inside, slams the door. A silence.

Marbles uses the piano to respond to the slamming door. Orest opens the door. They glare at each other. Orest slams the door again. Marbles again playfully punctuates this, on the harmonica this time. And Orest opens the door yet again, wielding a frying pan. Marbles freezes. Orest goes back into his apartment, closes the door. Marbles bounces the red Super Ball to Rose. She catches it.)

ROSE: Why, thank you. I'm Rose.

(Marbles takes her hand, kisses it, playfully smooching quickly up her arm.)

(Retracting her arm) I was just waiting for Mr. O'Neill. I tried knocking on his door, but there was no answer.

(Marbles crosses to O'Neill's door and knocks a strange pattern. Moments later, a small manila envelope appears from under the door. Marbles opens it, removes a handful of keys, chooses one.)

Was that him?

(Marbles nods.)

Do you know him well?

(Marbles nods again.)

Then perhaps you can clear something up for me.

(Marbles nods again, eyebrows dancing. Rose beckons him to approach her. He does so.)

It is Eugene O'Neill who lives behind that door, right? The great Eugene O'Neill?

(Marbles nods.)

Did you read the newspapers today?

(Marbles shakes his head no.)

Well, Mr. Marbles, this morning it was reported in the newspapers that Eugene O'Neill passed away last night in a Boston hospital. There was a rather detailed obituary in today's *New York Times*, with his photograph and everything.

(Marbles makes a surprised face.)

It was in all the newspapers and it was on the radio, too. But I suspect it isn't true. I suspect that he's staged his own, well, *death* is the correct word I suppose, because—

(Marbles quickly raises a finger up to his lips to silence her.)

Oh my goodness, have I said too much?

(He nods, very serious, grabs the shoe box.)

What's in the shoe box?

(He opens the lid, closes it very quickly.)

That's a rat!!!

(Marbles nods excitedly, but tries to ease her by petting the top of the box.)

Oh, it's a pet. I'm so sorry.

(He gives her the shoe box to hold while he opens the door to Unit Nine. Then he stares out into space near Rose with a look of horror on his face. When Rose turns to the apartment he quickly slips the small envelope of keys inside the piano bench. Then he returns for the shoe box, makes a gesture as if to say, "You'll have to excuse me," crosses back to Unit Nine, opens the door, enters with the shoe box, then closes the door behind him.)

(To herself, intense) This is your chance, Rose Hathaway! This is your big chance! Now get yourself together!

(She sets her hat, coat and purse on the piano, turns to O'Neill's door, and begins the following stitched-together monologue from Part III, Scene IV of Eugene O'Neill's Desire Under the Elms.*)*

(Suddenly wild) "I killed him, I tell ye! I smothered him. Go up an' see if ye don't b'lieve me!"

(She turns away, then whirls back on an invisible scene partner.)

"Don't ye dare tech me! What right hev ye t' question me 'bout him? He wa'n't yewr son! Think I'd have a son by yew? I'd die fust! I hate the sight o' ye an' allus did! It's yew I should've murdered, if I'd had good sense! I hate ye! I love Eben. I did from the fust. An' he was Eben's son— mine an' Eben's—not your'n!"

(Jerry Walsh enters, ascending the stairwell, undetected. He is late twenties, quietly eccentric, dark-haired, distinctly Italian-looking, clean-shaven, somewhat boyish. He wears nondescript clothes, more blue-collar than stylish, a jacket and thick-rimmed glasses. He is carrying two paper sacks of groceries, stops, watches Rose.

Rose senses someone behind her, stops the monologue, turns.)

JERRY: Don't stop on account of me.

(Rose says nothing.)

What was that?
ROSE: It's an audition piece. From a play. I'm so embarrassed.
JERRY: No, don't be embarrassed. What's the play?
ROSE: *Desire Under the Elms* by Eugene O'Neill. Do you know it?
JERRY: I certainly know the playwright.

ROSE: The piece I was performing takes place during the final
    scene. The character's name is Abbie Putnam and she
    confesses to killing her own child. It was inspired by the
    Greeks.

JERRY: Do the Greeks kill their children?

ROSE: What I mean to say is that O'Neill was inspired by clas-
    sic Greek drama. Playwrights like Sophocles, for instance,
    wrote about such things, and O'Neill was—*is*—very inter-
    ested in bringing these myths to the modern world. I played
    Abbie Putnam in a university production a few years ago.
    Although it was definitely in some ways emotionally chal-
    lenging to visit such dark places, I found it very freeing to
    express such intensity of feeling. Abbie's supposed to be
    thirty-five, so it was a bit of a stretch.

JERRY: How old are you?

ROSE: Twenty-five. But great writing and a little makeup can
    help to transcend one's age.

(He crosses stage left, toward Unit Nine, stops, turns to Rose.)

JERRY: So why are you here, do you know someone in the
    building?

ROSE: I'm waiting for Mr. O'Neill.

JERRY: The super.

ROSE: Yes, well . . .

JERRY: Well, what? He is the super.

ROSE: Of course he is . . . Do you live in the building?

JERRY: I do, yes.

ROSE: Have you had many dealings with Mr. O'Neill?

JERRY: When my windows won't shut or when the hot water isn't
    working.

ROSE: Do you know him on a personal level?

JERRY: I can't say that I do. He sort of keeps to himself . . . Are
    you looking to rent an apartment? Because if you are, you're
    wasting your time. The only unit that's vacant is this one
    here and it's supposed to be haunted by a man who killed

himself over twenty years ago. Poor bastard lost everything in the Great Crash. Apparently you can still see a portion of the noose hanging from a hook in the ceiling.

ROSE: I'm here on another matter.

JERRY: Personal business?

ROSE: Yes, actually.

JERRY: Can I ask how you got in the building?

ROSE: The door was ajar.

JERRY: I'm Jerry, by the way. Jerry Walsh.

ROSE: Pleased to meet you, Mr. Walsh. I'm Rose. Rose Hathaway.

JERRY: Rose, I apologize if I seem suspicious, but there've been some fishy dealings around here lately.

ROSE: Fishy meaning what?

JERRY: This guy has been coming by a lot. Wears nice clothes. Speaks in a certain way.

ROSE: Does he play the piano?

JERRY: Not that I know of. Why?

ROSE: Because the gentleman who lives in Apartment Nine is quite the piano player and he certainly has a peculiar way of communicating.

JERRY: *I* live in Apartment Nine.

ROSE: You do?

JERRY: Yes.

ROSE: Oh.

(He sets the groceries on the piano bench, moves quickly to Unit Nine's door.)

JERRY: Did someone go into my apartment?

ROSE: I think so, yes. Just a few minutes ago, in fact. *(Grows suddenly distrustful of herself)* . . . But maybe I was mistaken.

(Jerry produces keys from his pocket, attempts to key into his apartment.)

JERRY: The damn key isn't working.

(He tries again, starts to panic. He turns to Mr. O'Neill's apartment, starts to pound on his door.)

Mr. O'Neill! Mr. O'Neill, are you in there?!

(He pounds, he waits. Nothing.)

Mr. O'Neill!!! *(To Rose)* Bastard changed the locks again. *(To the door)* Mr. O'Neill, you have no right to change my locks! I paid you on time this month. You have no right! *(To Rose)* Cheap bastard. Did you really see someone go into my apartment?

ROSE: To be honest, I'm not entirely sure. He could have just as easily went down the stairs. It was all very confusing.

JERRY: Those stairs there?

ROSE: Are there other stairs?

JERRY: There's the fire escape.

ROSE: I think it was those stairs, but I'm not entirely certain.

JERRY: Well, there's no way he got in with a key because THE SUPER CHANGED THE LOCKS AGAIN, THE CREEP! You know, there should be some sort of a tenant's union that protects us from this kind of crap!!! I had my whole evening planned. I went out and bought all of these groceries! *(Handing her his handkerchief)* Your fingers are bleeding by the way.

ROSE: Oh, dear.

(She accepts the handkerchief. He crosses to his door, presses his ear to it, listens.)

Thank you . . . Nerves. I can't help but pick at them sometimes. My husband . . .

JERRY *(Still at the door)*: Your husband?

ROSE: He doesn't like it when I pick at my fingers. It upsets him terribly.

(Jerry goes into one of his grocery bags, retrieves a small sack of caramels, offers one to Rose.)

No, thank you.

(Just as he turns away, Rose attempts to return his handkerchief, but Jerry doesn't see this and she has to keep it. Jerry busies himself with his sack of caramels. After a silence:)

Are you married?

JERRY: Me? No.

ROSE: Is there a special someone in your life?

JERRY: Not really. I'm in love with a woman. She lives upstairs with her sister in Apartment Twelve. I actually saved her life.

ROSE: Oh.

JERRY: She stumbled in front of a subway car.

ROSE: And you caught her?

JERRY: On the uptown platform at the Delancey Street station. Grabbed her around the waist and pulled her back just as the express train was rushing by.

ROSE: Goodness. She must be so grateful.

JERRY: She hates me. Won't even give me a second glance.

ROSE: Maybe she's embarrassed.

JERRY: That she stumbled? People stumble all the time.

ROSE: Nearly stumbling onto the tracks in front of a speeding subway car could be quite, well, humiliating. Especially if there were people around.

JERRY: She's not embarrassed. She's suffered enough embarrassment already.

ROSE: How so?

(Jerry produces a pack of cigarettes, lights one, smokes.)

JERRY: She was involved in a scandalous affair. She was to be married to a rich man who was much older than her. She was caught with a younger man and there were photographs published in the newspapers. It's a long story. And I don't care, I love her anyway. The truth is that I somehow disgust her and I can't quite figure out why. She treats me like a nuisance.

ROSE: Have you spent any real time with her?

JERRY: No.

ROSE: Then how do you know you're in love with her?

JERRY: Because I ache all over. If I see her my heart nearly leaps out of my chest.

ROSE: There's a difference between love and fascination.

JERRY: Those are just words. There is not a phrase known to man that can articulate what I feel for this woman.

ROSE: Have you ever asked her out on a date?

JERRY: I've asked her to marry me four times.

ROSE: Well, that's quite extreme.

JERRY: I know, but I can't help it. The words fly out of my mouth. I've never known such madness.

ROSE: What's her name?

JERRY: Mary Seagrave. But it's spelled S-a-o-g-r-a-o-b-h. The Gaelic pronunciation is *Shougrauve*. Mary *Shougrauve*.

(He acts as if he's suddenly seized with some terribly blissful headache.)

ROSE: Are you all right?

JERRY: I dream about her every night. We're together on ocean liners. We're walking hand in hand through Central Park. We're on safari riding on the back of the same elephant. Sometimes I think I can feel her heart beating in my head. I suffer but she thinks I'm an insect.

ROSE: Mr. Walsh, have you entertained the thought that perhaps she wasn't stumbling on that subway platform?

JERRY: What are you implying? She stumbled. I saw it with my own two eyes.

ROSE: Of course you did.

JERRY: Why the hell would someone waste fifteen cents on the subway if they wanted to kill themselves? It would be so much easier to just walk off the Brooklyn Bridge. People stumble.

ROSE: I certainly stumble all the time. In fact, I nearly stumbled walking up those stai—

JERRY: You know, when I first started talking to you I thought you were almost pretty, but you're not. You nearly are, but something's missing.

ROSE: Is it my cheeks? Are my cheeks too pale?

(She removes a compact from her purse, brushes rouge on her cheeks.)

I'm sorry if I've agitated you, Mr. Walsh. I'm probably wrong about your friend. She very likely did stumble.

JERRY *(Stubbing his cigarette out in an ashtray on the hood of the piano)*: If we're going to be stuck together I would prefer that we change the subject.

(The pay phone rings. Jerry answers it.)

(Into phone) Hello? . . . Have some decency!!! Get a job, sir!!!

(He hangs up.)

Savages!

ROSE: Who was that?

JERRY: Witch hunters. With all of the recent hullabaloo about the Rosenbergs, the neighborhood has become quite aggressive, and in my opinion, unnecessarily paranoid.

(From the stairwell, Marbles throws a handful of marbles down the hall and disappears. Rose jumps.)

Nice try, Marbles! Don't think I didn't see that! *(To Rose)* Building prankster thinks he's so clever.

(He picks up a marble, hurls it toward the stairwell, starts picking up all the marbles over the following:)

ROSE: You know, I was almost cast in one of his plays?

JERRY: Whose plays?

ROSE: Eugene O'Neill's. It was the revival of *Anna Christie*. One of his greatest works. It won the 1922 Pulitzer Prize for Drama.

JERRY: Yeah, I saw the movie. "Garbo Talks."

ROSE: Yes, well that was the "movie."

JERRY: Why weren't you cast in the "play"?

ROSE: The role was given to an actress with more professional experience. I was called back twice, though. And I did meet him. He even stood up when I walked into the room and took my hand. It was quite a thrill for me.

JERRY: I imagine it was.

ROSE: He's very handsome for an older man. And so well-dressed.

JERRY: Are you aware that he was a friend of the Communist Party?

ROSE: Was he really?

JERRY: He was very close with John Reed, the party founder here in the United States. There was even a time when O'Neill had a romantic relationship with Reed's wife, Louise Bryant. He's still highly regarded by the current party.

ROSE: How do you know all of this?

JERRY *(Barreling on)*: When I was an undergraduate student I used to come into the city all the time to see plays. I think my favorite was *Summer and Smoke* by Tennessee Williams.

ROSE: I love Tennessee Williams! Not as much as Eugene O'Neill, but he's also very good.

JERRY: I saw *Summer in Smoke* three times in one week. My classmates thought I was crazy. I fell head-over-heels in love with the actress Monica Boyar.

ROSE: Where'd you go to school?

JERRY: Princeton University. I spent many hours on that train to New York.

ROSE: It must have been wonderful knowing you were going to see such an exciting play.

JERRY: What would we do without drama?

ROSE: A great theatrical work can change you, it really can.

JERRY: When it's good there's nothing like it.

ROSE: It's like a cleansing.

JERRY: I couldn't agree more.

ROSE: I wish my husband felt this way.

JERRY: He's not the artistic type, I gather.

ROSE: He thinks theater is an inconsequential entertainment. To him Eugene O'Neill, and Tennessee Williams are no different than Red Skelton or the Rockettes.

JERRY: I'm sorry to hear that. It must be frustrating for you.

ROSE: He can be a good sport about it. He does bring me into the city to see plays. He often falls asleep before the intermission but he tries his best.

(Beat.)

JERRY: Rose, can I share something with you? I realize we've just met, but I feel like I can trust you.

ROSE: Sure.

JERRY: I belong to a group of people much like us who believe in many of the same things we were just discussing, particularly in the power of collective transformation and communal responsibility. It's full of artists and writers and actors and poets.

ROSE: It sounds wonderful. Is it a drama club?

JERRY: No. But there are many involved with it who greatly appreciate the theater. We meet once a week right here on the Lower East Side. Our next meeting is actually tonight. In fact, I'm in charge of bringing food. That's what all these groceries are for. I'm making a big stew. Beef braised in

Barolo wine. With carrots and celery and garlic. You should come as my guest.

ROSE: Do you meet at a theater?

JERRY: We have in the past, yes, but the location changes. Tonight we're meeting at a friend's place a few blocks away.

ROSE: Is it some sort of salon?

JERRY: Not exactly. But many of its members could easily be found at a salon.

ROSE: It sounds so secretive.

(He checks the stairwell, then reaches into his pocket, produces a pamphlet, hands it to her.)

(Reading the pamphlet) "On Guard Against Browdersim, Titoism and Trotskyism" by John Gates. Who's John Gates?

JERRY: Only one of the greatest minds in American history. There's a rumor that he will be at tonight's meeting.

ROSE: Do you think Eugene O'Neill will be there?

JERRY: Very possibly.

ROSE: Mr. Walsh, I have to ask: Is this some sort of political club?

JERRY: It is, yes.

ROSE: Full of actors, writers and poets?

JERRY: And other people, too. Laborers, students, schoolteachers. People who are dissatisfied with the current state of things and hungry for something new.

ROSE *(Studying it further)*: This says it's an official pamphlet of the Young Communist League.

(The sound of a mousetrap snapping from the stairwell.)

Mr. Walsh, are you a Communist?

(He shushes her. She tries to return the pamphlet.)

JERRY: Keep it.

(She hesitates, then puts it in her purse.)

I promise you, Rose, Eugene O'Neill would be proud.

(Rose goes into her purse, produces a cigarette case, removes a cigarette.)

ROSE: . . . Anyway, as I was telling you earlier, I came very close to the title role in *Anna Christie* but they wound up giving it to a more experienced actress. But Mr. O'Neill wrote me a very nice letter after my second callback. Which was certainly encouraging to say the least.

JERRY: And wouldn't it be wonderful if he happened to be at tonight's meeting?

(Jerry lights her cigarette.)

ROSE *(A desperate need to change the subject)*: So Mr. Walsh, what is it exactly that do you do for a living, anyway?

JERRY: I work in the subway tunnels.

ROSE: I understand that's quite dangerous.

JERRY: It's okay, actually. With the CTA taking over this past June, there have been safety improvements. Accidental deaths are down. There have been far fewer electrocutions. The worst of it is the rats. I don't like rats so much.

ROSE: Do they bite?

JERRY: They bite, they jump, they do cartwheels. Have you ever seen a rat squeeze through a hole?

ROSE: I can't say that I have.

JERRY: They can wriggle themselves through the smallest holes because they're all cartilage. Holes the size of a subway token.

(He produces the new subway token, holds it up for her to see. He tosses it to her. She catches it.)

Hey, look at you, Pee Wee Reese.

(She attempts to return the token.)

That one's on the CTA.

ROSE: You're obviously very brave.

JERRY: You get used to rats just like anything else . . . You're surprised by my vocation.

ROSE: Well, as a graduate of Princeton . . .

JERRY: You assumed I had a job in business . . . Not all Ivy Leaguers head straight for Wall Street. I had opportunities to go that route. Or to medical school, for that matter, but I chose to be among the labor class. It's where I feel most comfortable. The important thing is to work and make a difference, no matter how small.

ROSE: It must be quite satisfying to feel so fulfilled.

JERRY *(Approaching the mousetrap)*: I'm helping the common man. Those who can't afford the luxuries of taxies and limousines and chauffeurs. My fellow workers.

(Jerry seizes the mousetrap, opens the window, throws it down to the courtyard.

Rose extinguishes her cigarette in the ashtray, goes into her purse, produces a letter, crosses to Jerry.)

ROSE: This is the letter that Mr. O'Neill wrote me.

(She hands the letter to him. He removes the letter from its envelope, studies it.)

JERRY: He has fascinating handwriting.

ROSE: Doesn't he, though?

JERRY *(Reading on, walking toward O'Neill's door)*: He was so impressed with you, Rose. This must have been very encouraging.

ROSE: It really was.

JERRY: Would you consider bringing this to tonight's meeting?

ROSE: Do you really think Mr. O'Neill might show?

JERRY: Anything's possible, Rose. But even if he doesn't, it would be a wonderful thing to share with the group.

(Suddenly a large crash from Unit Seven, and then intense moaning in Russian. Moments later, the door to Unit Seven opens and Orest rushes into the hallway in a panic.)

OREST: Neighbor Jerry! The bed collapse and my mother fall to floor and smash many many things. She nearly crush my Dansette record player and several vinyl jazz recordings! Can you please help me get the fat cow off floor?! She is very very fat and smell like explosion of shit from pig! I cannot do this with myself!

JERRY *(To Rose)*: Excuse me, Rose.

(Jerry and Orest exit into the Fedatovs' apartment, leaving the door open. Marbles appears from the stairwell, whistles to Rose, then shoots her with a toy popgun. She plays along. He shoots her two more times and she falls to the floor, creating a dramatic death scene. She convulses a bit in good fun. When she looks up he is gone.

A crazy sound comes from Unit Seven. Rose rises from the floor, and looks through the door from the hallway. Jerry Walsh and Orest can be heard grunting and hoisting Mrs. Fedatov off the floor. It takes a great effort, with Mrs. Fedatov crying out in Russian throughout.

While this is going on, the door to Unit Nine opens. Marbles sneaks out, holding Jerry Walsh's Magnavox Envoy twenty-one-inch television set. He has fashioned an odd aluminum foil wig on his head. He turns to O'Neill's door, quietly taps a code. The door opens. Marbles gives the television to O'Neill, and the envelope of keys from before. Then the door closes.

Marbles moves to the piano bench, reaches into Rose's handbag, removes Jerry Walsh's handkerchief, places a large "shooter" marble in it, grabs Jerry Walsh's groceries from off the top of the piano, tiptoes past Rose, then chucks the handkerchief rocket toward O'Neill's door, where it makes a loud thud. Rose turns to the sound and Marbles sneaks past her with Jerry's groceries, and disappears down the stairwell.

Rose crosses to the handkerchief and the "shooter" marble, confused.

Jerry Walsh reemerges, out of breath and amazed. Rose places the "shooter" marble and the handkerchief in her purse.)

That is the largest human being I have ever seen in my life.

ROSE: What's wrong with her?

JERRY: I don't know, but whatever it is has made her enormous.

(Orest enters the hallway, also out of breath.)

OREST: Neighbor Jerry . . . I thank you from basement of my heart . . . I apologize in behalf of my mother and my country . . . This is truly embarrassment situation . . . For your help, I will gladly clean your toilet and your refrigerator . . .

JERRY: Orest, I was happy to help.

OREST: I will clean your toilet, your refrigerator, and I will wash in the laundromat all of your socks.

JERRY: That's really not necessary, Orest.

OREST: We shall discuss this matter on another time, Neighbor Jerry.

JERRY: Very well.

OREST: Thank you again.

JERRY: You're welcome.

OREST: Hello, Rose Hathaway. Good afternoon.

ROSE: Good afternoon, Orest.

OREST: Enjoy this great man.

(Orest goes into his apartment and closes the door.)

ROSE: Jerry, do you still have my letter?

(He pulls it out of his back pocket, hands it to her. It is a bit smashed and fouled. She is pretty devastated. Jerry's hands are soiled. Rose returns his handkerchief, keeps the marble.

Megan Ridgley, Mary's sister, enters, ascending the stairwell. She is late twenties, dressed for cold weather, carrying a bag of groceries.)

JERRY: Hi, Megan.

MEGAN: Hello, Jerry.

JERRY: This is Rose.

MEGAN: Hello, Rose.

ROSE: Hello, Megan.

JERRY *(To Rose)*: Megan is Mary's sister, the woman I was telling you about. *(To Megan)* Mr. O'Neill changed the locks again.

(Megan runs upstairs, tries to key in, curses, kicks the door, curses, "Darnit," returns without her groceries, holding her sister's coat.)

MEGAN: Have you seen Mary?

JERRY: I'm afraid I haven't.

MEGAN: She hasn't come home for two days. We were supposed to have Thanksgiving together. I'm tempted to file a missing persons report with the police. She left her coat in front of our door. You sure you haven't seen her?

JERRY *(Mesmerized by the coat)*: Megan, you know all too well that if she would allow me, I would see Mary as much as possible.

MEGAN *(To Rose)*: Have you seen a tall woman with red hair? Very pretty?

ROSE: I'm afraid I haven't.

(Jerry Walsh's apartment door opens, Orest entering the hallway, triumphant.)

OREST: Neighbor Jerry!

JERRY: Orest, what are you doing in my apartment?

OREST: I can explain, Neighbor Jerry. I make very risky move across ledge of building and with much effort and cunning I am able to open your window. You are locked out and it is least I can't do for your assistance with my fat mother.

MEGAN: Orest, did something happen to your mother?

OREST: The horrible beast fall to floor and practically destroy building, but Neighbor Jerry is kind enough to borrow his assistance. She is fine now.

MEGAN: And so you returned the favor by risking your life on the ledge of the building?

OREST: It is not so high up.

JERRY: Orest, you really didn't have to do that.

OREST: It is my revenge for your charity. Please go forward, fine chum, and enjoy your evening. It's the least I can't do.

JERRY (*Looking around, confused*): Where did my groceries go?

ROSE: I thought you left them on top of the piano.

JERRY: Marbles! Marbles, that's not funny! I really need those groceries! I was going to make a stew! (*To Megan*) If you find your sister, please give her my best.

MEGAN: I will.

JERRY: Rose, please don't leave without saying good-bye.

ROSE: I won't, Mr. Walsh. Thank you for the conversation.

(*Jerry exits into his apartment, closes the door. Orest takes a few careful steps toward his own apartment.*)

MEGAN: Orest, I bought some pork chops and applesauce at the supermarket. Would you like to join me for dinner? I realize I'm obviously locked out, but if you wouldn't mind lending me your kitchen—

OREST: No, thank you, Megan. I have to practice for audition.

MEGAN: Will you be practicing all night?

OREST: Yes. It is very difficult piece.

MEGAN: Do you take a break?

OREST: I cannot take break.

MEGAN: Is it because of your mother? I'd be happy to cook enough for her, too. I have plenty of food.

OREST: There is never enough food for her. She is fat like whale and she smells like a garbage truck with shit from a man encased in it. No thank you very much.

MEGAN: It's Saturday night, Orest. Your audition is three days away.

OREST: I must strengthen my lip. It is weak.

MEGAN: I would have to disagree.

OREST: My lip is weak, Megan! It is weak, okay?! I can feel how weak it is as I am talking to you!

(He grabs his lip and stretches it oddly.)

You see?! Weak lip!

(Jerry bursts into the hallway again.)

JERRY: My TV is gone! My Magnavox twenty-one-inch Envoy television set is gone! And so are my leftovers from Thanksgiving and a jar of lima beans! And two bags of groceries that I bought not even an hour ago! What the hell is going on in this building? Is someone playing a practical joke on me? Megan, has your sister hired someone to toy with me? I realize she hates me, but I would say this is taking it too far. This kind of thing is liable to drive a person mad!

MEGAN: Jerry, Mary hasn't hired anyone to do any such thing.

(He festers for a moment and then:)

JERRY: Why won't she marry me?!

MEGAN: Because she doesn't love you.

JERRY: But she won't even give me a chance! Is it because I'm not interested in playing bridge in East Hampton or spending weekends on the Jersey shore with all of those rich fools?!

Those withering lobsters parading around in their Coupe de
Villes and Eldorados?! I'm an educated man, Megan. I went
to Princeton University!

*(He exits into his apartment, then quickly returns with a
framed certificate.)*

I could have gone to medical school! I graduated magna
cum laude! I *choose* to work in the subway tunnels—
I *choose* to do that! To work among the common people is
important to me! To work! That doesn't mean I don't have
something to offer a woman! That doesn't mean a man
doesn't have character or so much love in his heart it could
burst! Your sister didn't even go to college! In fact, she
can't even get a job as a secretary! You know how I know?
Because I followed her to an interview at Sullivan and
Cromwell last week. I walked all the way down to Broad
Street. I watched her stop and feed the pigeons on the corner of Canal and Church. And I saw her buy a pretzel off
of a wagon two blocks later! And she went back to him
for mustard and a napkin! And I saw her check her reflection in the window of a parked cab on Duane Street.
I watched her all the way to Broad Street. I spied on your
sister!

MEGAN: How do you know she didn't get the job?
JERRY: I just know, okay? *(Exasperated)* . . . I saved her life,
Megan.
MEGAN: Yes, Jerry, everyone in this city knows how you saved
my sister's life! I think my sixth graders up in the Bronx
even know . . . What are you holding?
JERRY: My degree from Princeton University.
MEGAN: What are you going to do with that?
JERRY: I'm going to smash it.
MEGAN: Why?
JERRY: Because it means nothing! I'm going to smash it over my
head!

(He moves to smash it. He can't. He simply grips it, squeezing so tightly that his hands nearly burst. He stops, hugs it to his chest, sinks to the floor, drained.)

MEGAN: Jerry, can I give you some friendly advice?

JERRY: . . . What.

MEGAN: Stop hounding her. Give her some space. Don't spy on her. Don't follow her around. Don't do any of that.

JERRY: For how long?

MEGAN: I would wait a month. Or two. At least.

JERRY: And then what?

MEGAN: Then maybe try writing her a letter.

JERRY: Does she enjoy receiving letters?

MEGAN: Who doesn't like a nice letter?

JERRY: You really think that could work?

MEGAN: I think it's a better strategy than going to your knee and begging her to marry you every time she comes around the corner.

JERRY: I don't beg.

MEGAN: Yes you do, Jerry, and for a woman there's nothing worse. You beg at her like a dog. It's pathetic.

JERRY: What do you think, Orest? Should I write Mary a letter?

OREST: I think women are very irritating creatures. Like a rash in the pants. They need so much attentions. Special kisses. Hugs all the time. Candies and prizes. They are nuisance and most of the time ruin your life and should be killed. In Russia, many, many women are killed for these purposes.

JERRY: Okay, I'll write her a letter then. Do you think she'd actually read it?

MEGAN: I think she would, yes.

JERRY: I love her so much, Megan. From the moment she stumbled on the subway platform . . . I grabbed her around the waist . . . The express train rushing by . . . She gave herself to me . . . Right there in my arms, she surrendered. It was the smallest thing but I've never known anything more definite.

MEGAN: You don't even know her, Jerry.

JERRY: I want to, though. I want to know her so badly . . . But I guess I'll wait. I'll wait and then I'll write her a brilliant letter.

OREST: You should sleep with whore in cheap hotel and go to horse races. Or maybe sleep with horse and drink many vodkas. Enjoy.

(Orest exits into his apartment.)

ROSE: Maybe you should call the police.

JERRY: The New York City Police Department is the most crooked organization there is, unfortunately. *(To Megan)* Thank you for your advice and your honesty, Megan. I wish you all a good evening.

(Jerry exits into his apartment with his degree from Princeton.)

ROSE: I agree with you one hundred percent. I think letter writing—even a short note—can make all the difference.

(Megan crosses to O'Neill's door, knocks, waits, nothing. Knocks again.)

MEGAN: Mr. O'Neill?

(She turns back to Rose.)

You mind me asking what you're doing here?

ROSE: I'm also waiting to speak with Mr. O'Neill.

MEGAN: About what?

ROSE: Last year he wrote me a letter complimenting me on an audition. I was called back twice and seriously considered for the part, but they ultimately went with a more experienced actress.

MEGAN: The playwright Eugene O'Neill wrote you a letter?

ROSE: Yes.

MEGAN: And you're waiting to speak with Mr. O'Neill who lives in Apartment Ten? Mr. O'Neill the super?

ROSE: I am. And I'll wait all night if I have to.

MEGAN: But Eugene O'Neill the playwright died last night.

ROSE: So they say.

MEGAN: Oh, so you think . . .

ROSE: That he staged the whole thing and that he's been living here incognito.

MEGAN: Honey, the Eugene O'Neill who lives in Apartment Ten is not Eugene O'Neill the playwright who died last night, I assure you.

ROSE: Yes he is.

MEGAN: Rose, I'm an English teacher. I've studied his plays.

ROSE: But of course his neighbors are going to cover for him. A man that important? I may be young, but I wasn't born yesterday.

MEGAN *(Polite)*: Excuse me.

(Megan pounds on O'Neill's door.)

Mr. O'Neill?! *(To Rose)* I gave him twenty dollars last week as a guarantee on the balance of the rent. He promised he wouldn't change the locks again. It's the third time this has happened since the rents were raised in June. *(To the door)* Mr. O'Neill!

ROSE: I don't think he's there.

MEGAN: The bastard's always there. He hardly ever leaves his apartment.

ROSE: Do you ever hear him working?

MEGAN: Working on what, a whiskey bottle?

ROSE: On his typewriter.

MEGAN: Typewriter? If the ogre even has a typewriter it's one he's confiscated. You should see all the things he has in there. Floor lamps, toaster ovens, a grandfather clock. The guy will take your salt-and-pepper shakers off your kitchen table. Just two months ago he keyed into Jerry Walsh's apartment and took his armchair because he was a day late with the rent. A day late! And then he wouldn't return it unless he paid him a two-dollar service fee. *(At O'Neill's door again)* Mr. O'Neill, if you're in there, I demand that you speak with me! That twenty dollars was a guarantee! You had no right to change my locks! *(To Rose)* If he ever comes out of there you'll see that the person who lives behind that door is just an angry old man with halitosis.

(Megan relents, feels the cold radiator.)

Good night.

(Megan sits on the radiator, slumped, exhausted.)

ROSE: So you're a schoolteacher?
MEGAN: If that's what you want to call it. Just getting control of my class takes everything I have. There isn't actually any teaching going on. I feel like I'm wrangling chimpanzees. It's the Saturday following Thanksgiving and I'm still exhausted.
ROSE: And you teach English?
MEGAN: Yeah, English. When I took the job I had this romantic vision of discussing Edgar Allan Poe and Chaucer. I can't even get them to read a comic book.

(Suddenly, several eggs smash up against the window. Both women jump.)

Jesus!
ROSE: Who's throwing eggs?
MEGAN: Who knows? I'm sure it has something to do with us having Russians living in the building. Those damn trials have everyone believing they're all spies and murderers.

I can't imagine what Orest and his mother are going through right now. In general, this building is really starting to give me the creeps.

ROSE: Earlier Jerry was telling me about the man who hanged himself.

MEGAN: Yeah, you couldn't pay me to go into that apartment. I keep hearing murmurings that it's going to be rented out. I certainly wouldn't want to live in there.

ROSE: How long have you lived in the building?

MEGAN: It'll be four years in January. My sister moved in with me in September.

ROSE *(Noticing her wedding band)*: And you're married . . .

MEGAN: I was. He died in the war.

ROSE: I'm so sorry.

MEGAN: It was nine years ago this past June. We were barely married six months before he was shipped off to Normandy.

ROSE: That must have been devastating.

MEGAN: He served his country and now he's buried in his uniform in Arlington, Virginia.

ROSE: What was his name?

MEGAN: Corporal Charles Guyton Ridgley. We were high school sweethearts back in Oak Park, Illinois.

ROSE: You must miss him terribly.

MEGAN: After the funeral I used to think I'd see him on the street. Or sitting in a café. Or doing the crossword puzzle at the other end of a subway car. I'd write Charlie letters and send them to the address where we lived with his parents in Chicago.

ROSE: You were so in love with him.

MEGAN: Yeah, I fell in love with a soldier. Just my luck. Charlie was so gung ho about serving his country. Are you married?

ROSE: Yes . . . I think Richard would like me to . . . I want to be an actress. No let me correct that: I *am* an actress . . . We're from Madison, Wisconsin. We went to school there, and were married shortly after graduation. Richard got a job offer from Metropolitan Life Insurance so we moved out

here. Well, to Darien, Connecticut to be exact. I've always
wanted to live in New York City. I've dreamed of performing
on Broadway since I was a little girl.

MEGAN: Well, there is still time to do all that.

ROSE: I suppose that's true.

(Rose is visibly upset now.)

I can't even imagine what that must have been like . . .

MEGAN: What what must have been like?

ROSE: Losing the man you love.

MEGAN: Eventually all of that fades and you get on with your life.

*(Megan moves close to Rose. She offers her a tissue from her
pocket.)*

ROSE: Thank you.

*(Megan tidies the mess of cigarette butts on the hood of the
piano.)*

Has there been anyone else?

MEGAN: Well, Orest, actually. But things have been strained
lately, and I'm not sure why. Not even a month ago, on Hal-
loween, we went up to the roof and had the most wonderful
time. We told each other so many things. He told me about
his family in Russia and how difficult it was to get to America, and I told him about losing Charlie . . . and it was really
lovely. He even played his horn for me . . . and we kissed.

(Suddenly, Orest's door flies opens.)

OREST: I do not love you, Megan. There are many men to make a
wife for in New York. Perhaps you go look for nice man in
Central Park. Or at Grand Central Station railroad.

MEGAN: Okay.

OREST: That night on roof was not real. It was phony baloney.

MEGAN: It felt real to me.

OREST: But in my brain it were like torture chamber. It were very foolish of me and I lie to myself. You are ugly woman, Megan. You have shit for face and mouth like cuckoo clock. And you are too skinny. I like pretty woman. And I like woman who is more fat. I would like to be with woman who has beautiful face and big chubby stomach and no shit for brains. Good night. I hope you get syphilis. *(To Rose)* Rose Hathaway, you have very pretty face. And eyes like leopard. Enjoy.

(He turns, goes back into his apartment, closes the door behind him.

Megan is shocked. She quietly cries.

Louie Zappaleo enters, ascending the stairwell. He is Italian, forties, well-dressed in a suit and tie, and nice hat and overcoat. He is carrying the same pigeon that Marbles released out the window.

Just as Rose moves to comfort Megan:)

LOUIE: Ladies . . . How are you, this evening?

ROSE: Fine, thank you.

(Marbles appears from the stairwell. Louie hands Marbles the pigeon. Marbles exits.)

LOUIE: Is Mr. O'Neill around?

MEGAN: That seems to be the question of the night.

LOUIE: The man is in high demand. *(Knocking; to the door)* Mr. O'Neill, you come back to life yet? It's Louie Zappaleo. I'd like to have a moment of your time, please.

(Louie produces a pack of Viceroys.)

(To Megan) Cigarette?

MEGAN: No, thank you.

LOUIE *(To Rose)*: Miss?

ROSE *(Accepting the cigarette)*: Yes, thank you.

(Just as Louie is about to light Rose's cigarette, the sound of three gunshots comes from Jerry Walsh's apartment.
Jerry comes out into the hallway holding a pistol.)

JERRY: Goddamn rat in my kitchen! A rat! That's not sanitary! It's downright disgusting! I pay a hundred and five dollars rent—on time, mind you—and what do I get in return?! I get my locks changed and I get a goddamn rat in my kitchen!!! *(To Louie)* You're that guy.

LOUIE: What guy?

JERRY: The well-dressed mystery man.

LOUIE: Well, I appreciate the compliment, Mr. Walsh.

JERRY: How do you know my name?

LOUIE: I know a lot of people's names in the neighborhood.

JERRY: Why?

LOUIE: Why? Because I'm a neighborhood kind of guy and I make it my business. I know the men down at the barbershop. I know the deli owners and diner waitresses. I'm friendly with the police precinct. The cabbies. The hobos. I also happen to know that your real name is Giuseppe, Mr. Walsh.

JERRY: Giuseppe?

LOUIE: Giuseppe Mascagne to be exact. As a fellow Italian I have no idea why you would want to change your name to Jerry Walsh. That's a beautiful name you got there. Why would you want to change it? *(To Megan)* Curious, don't you think?

MEGAN: Everyone has their own reasons for doing things.

LOUIE: You're absolutely right. Seagrave, isn't it? Oh no, you're Ridgley. Your sister's Seagrave. Pretty Gaelic name. *(To Jerry)* You mind lowering that gun for me, Giuseppe?

(Jerry lowers the gun.)

Thank you.

(The Fedatov door opens. Orest stands there with his arms raised.)

OREST: TAKE ME G-R-U! TAKE ME N-K-V-D. TAKE ME TO GULAG AND DESTROY MY LIFE!

(Mr. O'Neill's door opens. O'Neill stands there in his boxer shorts and wife-beater. Mary comes out from behind him, slowly, carefully. The back of her head and the back of her dress are covered in cat hair.)

O'NEILL: What the hell's goin' on out here?

LOUIE: Mr. O'Neill, so glad you could join us.

JERRY: Mary.

MARY: Hello, Jerry.

JERRY: Mary Saograobh.

MARY: Jerry Walsh.

JERRY: I shot a rat, Mary. Right in my kitchen. I got him on the first shot. And then I got him again. And again. It's the first time I shot anything and it felt wonderful.

MARY: Congratulations. Maybe you should go back in your apartment and shoot yourself. Or if you want more of a build you could go rat, dog, monkey, a small child, a pygmy, and then yourself.

MEGAN: Mary, what are you doing in Mr. O'Neill's apartment?

MARY: We were just chatting.

MEGAN: About what?

MARY: We were discussing the lock situation.

MEGAN: Turn around.

MARY: Why?

MEGAN: Just turn around.

(Mary turns around.)

Is that cat hair all over your back?

(No answer.)

Mary, why is there cat hair all over your back?
o'neill: We were discussin' the lock situation.

(Awkward pause.)

louie: Speaking of the lock situation, I was just telling Giuseppe here about my appreciation for the neighborhood. Wouldn't you say that's true, Mr. O'Neill?
o'neill: Who the hell's Giuseppe?
louie: Mr. Walsh is Giuseppe. Isn't that something?
megan: Jerry, could you please put that gun away.
jerry: There's nothing to worry about. I'm out of bullets, see?

(He places it to his head, fires twice. Everyone is clearly startled. Hysteria.)

orest: Neighbor Jerry. Don't!

(Louie approaches Jerry, who still holds his pistol, sitting on the piano bench now, dejected.)

louie: Easy does it now, Giuseppe.

*(Louie opens the chamber of the pistol, removes a bullet, places it in his pocket.
    A tense lull.)*

Now that everyone is out in the hallway I'd like to extend a warm-hearted invitation to all of you to come visit my family's ravioli shop just around the corner on Houston Street.

(From his breast pocket, Louie removes a handful of takeout menus, starts passing them around.)

It's called Alida's Ravioli and I can guarantee the finest homemade pastas, sauces and raviolis in New York City. We got ravioli, cavatelli, manicotti, stuffed shell pasta, tortellini, three types of gnocchi, rigatoni, farfalle, all kinds of sauces, meatballs that'll make your heart ache. And hold on to your hats, we also have a seven-hundred-pound provolone cheese that just arrived on a steamship from Genoa, Italy. You like pasta, Giuseppe?

JERRY: I prefer stew.

LOUIE: Well I hope you like the view from your new living room windows, because those were installed by a good friend of mine, Joe Binobo. Skinny Joe Binobo, we call him. And I hope all of you appreciate the new cigarette machine I just had installed on the first floor. We got Pall Malls, Kents, Camels, Phillip Morris, Chesterfields, Lucky Strikes, Marlboros, and for you lovely ladies, Old Golds. My particular brand of choice happens to be Viceroys, but let's get back to pasta. *(To Rose)* What about you, young lady, you like pasta?

ROSE: I do, as a matter of fact, yes.

LOUIE: What's your favorite dish?

ROSE: I quite like linguini with clams, actually.

LOUIE: White or red sauce?

ROSE: White.

LOUIE: I didn't catch your name.

ROSE: Rose Hathaway.

LOUIE: Nice to meet you, Rose Hathaway. I'm Louie Zappaleo. Welcome to the neighborhood.

ROSE: Oh, I don't live here.

LOUIE: Who said you had to live here to feel included? Or to love pasta for that matter? Everyone loves pasta, right, Mr. O'Neill?

O'NEILL: I'm a ham on rye guy, but I like pasta, I do.

LOUIE: Well, there's always the special exception. Take me, for instance: I like a good peanut butter and jelly sandwich almost as much as my mother's fettuccini. Not quite as much, but it's certainly close. A peanut butter and jelly sandwich with an ice-cold glass of milk. What a dependable American staple. Peanut butter and jelly. Apple pie. Hamburgers and hot dogs at the Fourth of July barbecue. What about you, Mr. Fedatov, you and your mother enjoy a grade-A American all-beef hot dog now and then, or would you prefer a nice plate of spaghetti and meatballs? Fresh-grated parmesan. Or Pecorino Romano if you prefer that. A little garlic bread on the side?

OREST: My mother eats like wild elephant with horse living in her stomach. She eats many many dishes all the time, all the day and night: dishes consisting of tuna fish; dishes consisting of roast beef with horseradish; hearty pork stews; plates of cheeses and potatoes; kielbasa; borscht; chocolate cakes; oysters with crackers and pickled herring; vanilla puddings and baskets of pears; the head of pig; the tongue of cow; cotton candy from circus; raspberry ice cream and dishes of butterscotch candies; lamb chops and chocolate milk. Hamburgers with peanut butter. Many many apple pies. So many jellies. And perhaps one million hot dogs on the Fourth of July barbecue. All of this is very important to her. But her most favorite dish of all is spaghetti and meatballs and all the pastas and sauces from Alida's Ravioli.

LOUIE: Well how do you like that? And what about you lovely Seagrave girls? I'll bet you enjoy a nice, meaty lasagna now and then. Where are you ladies from anyway?

MEGAN: Oak Park, Illinois.

LOUIE: Oh, Oak Park, Illinois, very nice. By the way, how is that new bathtub working out, Megan? Better than the old one, I hope.

MEGAN: It's working very well, thank you.

JERRY: Why is it any of your business?

LOUIE: I don't know, Giuseppe—that's a very good question. Mr. O'Neill, maybe you can answer that for us. Why is Megan and Mary's new bathtub my business?

JERRY: Mr. Zappaleo, if you have something you want Mr. O'Neill to say, perhaps you should say it yourself.

LOUIE: You say you like stew, is that right, Giuseppe?

JERRY: I know what I don't like.

LOUIE: What goes into a good stew? Carrots, potatoes, celery . . . beef, Barolo wine.

JERRY *(To himself)*: He's doing it again, he's doing it again . . .

LOUIE: Plenty to go around for the common man.

(Jerry says nothing.)

Giuseppe, I just want to make sure everyone's happy, that's all. We live in one of the greatest neighborhoods in New York; one of the greatest in the world. How about it, Mr. Fedatov, you and your mother like the neighborhood?

OREST: Yes, thank you very much. We love America and the song "Star Spangled Banjo." We sing this excellent song every night before we go to sleep and twice in the morning.
    (Singing:)

Oh say can't you sing,
By the dawn's early life
What's so proudly we hail
For the firelight's last cleaning
Whose broad stripes and bright cars . . .

(Orest trails off, loses the song.)

LOUIE: Thanks, Mr. Fedatov. Keep up the good work.

OREST: Thank you, Mr. Zappaleo. And my mother thanks you in equal measurements.

(From off, we hear Orest's mother groan, "Thank you, Mr. Zappaleo.")

Enjoy.

(The pay phone rings. It rings again. Megan crosses to it, answers.)

MEGAN *(Into phone)*: Hello? . . . *(Turning to Jerry)* It's for you.

(Jerry crosses to the phone.)

JERRY *(Into phone)*: Hello? . . . Yes, this is he . . . Uh-huh . . . Uh-huh . . . Yes, I'll be there.

(He hangs up. A strained silence.)

LOUIE: What's going on, Giuseppe? . . . Special engagement? . . . You got tickets to the opera? Is the circus in town?

JERRY: Dinner at my mother's house.

LOUIE: Oh yeah? And where does she live?

JERRY: . . . Bensonhurst, Brooklyn.

LOUIE: Well, if your mother's Italian, and being from Bensonhurst I have a hunch she is, Giuseppe, I'm sure she likes pasta, and I'd be happy to send you on your way with a bottle or two of my mother's original ragu sauce.

JERRY *(Relenting)*: Thank you. That would be very nice.

LOUIE: I'll be sure to give my mother your name. Just stop by the shop in the next hour or so. *(To everyone)* Like I said, Alida's Ravioli is just around the corner on Houston Street. You don't wanna miss the seven-hundred-pound provolone cheese. You do not wanna miss that, no sir, no ma'am. I know my mother would love to see all of you . . .

MEGAN: We'll definitely come by.

LOUIE: Glad to hear that, Megan. Glad as a handshake, and these days there's not enough of those to go around, right Mr. Fedatov?

OREST: Enjoy.

LOUIE: Mr. O'Neill, you mind if we talk in private for a moment?

O'NEILL: What for?

LOUIE: I'd just like to sit down with you, have ourselves a chit-chat. A little bird told me that you're planning some sort of vacation to Miami Beach.

(From the stairwell, the sound of Marbles tweeting like a bird.)

O'NEILL: I'm not goin' nowhere.

LOUIE: Sure you are. That same little bird told me you bought a one-way ticket and that it's nicely hidden away under the ice cube trays in your freezer. I happen to know Miami Beach very well. I could give you some pointers on all the hot spots. Miami Beach is an exciting place right about now. How bout that, Miss Hathaway?

ROSE: I've never been to Florida.

LOUIE: What a shame. You should try it sometime. Put a little color in your cheeks . . .

(Rose touches her cheeks.)

Megan, Mary, Mr. Fedatov, Giuseppe, on behalf of the neighborhood I'd like to take a moment and apologize about the recent hike in rent. I hope the ninety-five dollars a month isn't too steep. If you're having any problems, Megan, Mary, Mr. Fedatov, Giuseppe, don't feel like you can't come talk to me. Louie Zap is your friend to the end.

MEGAN: Ninety-five dollars? I think you mean a hundred and five.

LOUIE: I believe ninety-five dollars is the correct amount.

MEGAN: Well, Mr. O'Neill's been collecting a hundred and five.

JERRY: For five months now.

LOUIE: Is that right, Mr. O'Neill?

O'NEILL: Hey, hey, hey now. Everything's goin' up.

LOUIE: Well, we'll have to talk about that. In addition to your Miami trip, that's something we'll definitely get to the bottom of. Right, Mr. O'Neill?

(O'Neill says nothing.)

How about that chat?

(O'Neill looks out at everyone, a pleading look. Louie opens the door to his apartment, O'Neill starts to follow him in.)

ROSE: Mr. O'Neill!

(O'Neill turns.)

I just wanted to thank you for your letter.

O'NEILL: What letter?

ROSE: The letter you wrote to me. I'm Rose Hathaway.

O'NEILL: I haven't written a letter in over twenty-five years.

(She offers him the envelope. He opens it, reads the letter.)

I didn't write this.

ROSE: But of course you did.

O'NEILL: That's my name and address, but I never wrote this letter.

ROSE: Sure you did . . . By the way, why'd you shave your mustache? I always thought it looked so handsome.

O'NEILL: I've never had a mustache, missy.

(Rose snatches the letter back and starts the same monologue as before, viciously and embroiled.)

ROSE: "I killed him, I tell ye! I smothered him. Go up an' see if ye don't b'lieve me! Don't ye dare tech me! What right hev ye t' question me 'bout him? He wa'n't yewr son! Think I'd have a son by yew? I'd die fust! I hate the sight o' ye an' allus did! It's yew I should've murdered, if I'd had good sense! I hate ye! I love Eben. I did from the fust. An' he was Eben's son—mine an' Eben's—not your'n!"

O'NEILL: Why are you so mad at me? I don't even know you.

ROSE *(Singing)*:

How much is that doggie in the window? —Arf arf—
The one with the waggily tail.
How much is that doggie in the window? —Arf arf—
I do hope that doggie's . . .

LOUIE *(Approaching Rose)*: Thanks for comin' in, sweetheart. We'll let you know.

(Louie pushes O'Neill into his apartment and closes the door. Rose is now spent, emptied of everything. She looks at the others, then slowly crosses to Jerry, reaches into her purse, removes the red pamphlet he had given her, and hands it back to him. He accepts it and stuffs it in his back pocket. Rose then crosses to the piano and pulls it away from condemned Unit Eight's door. She stands before the door a moment, turns the knob, and opens it. She then removes a marble from her purse—the one that rolled toward her at the beginning of the play—and places it very carefully on the floor. She then sets the envelope containing the letter on the hood of the piano. She enters the condemned apartment, closing the door behind her.

Megan, Mary, Orest and Jerry are left in the hall. There is a tense silence.

Marbles enters from the stairwell. He crosses to the piano, pushes it back in front of the door. He takes the envelope from the top of the piano. He stares at the others, one by one, then exits toward the stairwell, whistling "(How Much Is That) Doggie in the Window?"

Silence.

Mary retrieves her coat, crosses to Megan, starts to hand Megan the keys to their apartment, but Megan snatches them and slaps Mary. Mary turns and exits toward the stairwell with her coat. Jerry starts after her.)

JERRY: Mary.

MARY *(Wheeling sharply)*: STOP FOLLOWING ME!!!

(Mary completes her exit down the stairs. Jerry turns back to Megan, then to the stairs. He clutches the banister very intensely for a moment, fighting the urge to follow her, and then runs down the stairs after Mary.

*Megan and Orest are alone in the hallway. Moments later,
violence can be heard coming from behind Mr. O'Neill's door.
The sound of Mr. O'Neill pleading for his life. More violence.
Then silence.)*

MEGAN: Orest . . .

*(The pay phone rings. Megan lets it ring three or four times,
then answers the phone.)*

Hello? . . . I'm sorry? No, there are no Communists living in
the building. You obviously have the wrong number.

*(Megan hangs up. The phone rings again. She picks it up
very quickly and hangs up.)*

Orest . . .

*(He spits on the floor, then exits into his apartment. Megan
turns toward the piano, upset.
     Several moments later, Jerry enters, from the stairwell,
somewhat in shock. He is wet from the rain and holding
Mary's gold cigarette box.)*

JERRY: She got into a cab on Houston Street, heading west . . .
     I could see the back of her head. Her red hair . . . I could
     almost smell it. Like apples and licorice . . . She dropped
     her cigarettes.

*(He stares at the cigarette box in his hand.
     Megan crosses toward the stairwell.)*

MEGAN: Excuse me.

*(Jerry steps aside and Megan exits up the stairs. We hear her
keying into her apartment and the door closing. Jerry crosses
to the condemned apartment and stands in front of the door,*

*considers it, but then leaves the gold cigarette case on the top
of the piano, and exits into his apartment.*

*The hallway is empty for a moment. Then Unit Ten's door
opens and O'Neill enters carrying Jerry Walsh's television
set and Orest's toaster. Louie Zap follows him into the hall.
O'Neill's face is bloodied.*

*O'Neill places the television in front of Jerry Walsh's door
and the toaster in front of Orest's door. O'Neill then turns
and limps back into his apartment.*

*Louie takes the gold cigarette case off the piano and puts it
in his pocket. He then produces a plastic bag of marbles, walks
toward the stairwell and knocks on the window. The window
opens and Marbles appears. Louie hands him the bag of marbles. The window closes, and Louie exits down the stairs.*

*Richard Bumper enters. He is late twenties, wears lei-
surely clothes, a nice coat. He is carrying a leather briefcase. He looks at all the door numbers, studies them slowly,
curiously. He nearly slips on a marble, regains his balance,
reaches down, picks up a marble, places it in his pocket.*

*Richard Bumper makes his way upstage to O'Neill's
apartment. He knocks. No answer. He knocks again, looks
around. Still no answer. He takes a seat on the piano bench,
winds his watch.*

*Marbles emerges from the stairwell, but stays behind the
railing. He produces the half-smoked cigarette that Mary
had given him earlier. He produces a single wooden match,
strikes it, light the cigarette, smokes.*

*Richard Bumper turns to him. He rises off the piano bench
and approaches.)*

RICHARD: Hello. Dick Bumper, Metropolitan Life Insurance.

*(Richard produces a business card, offers it to Marbles. Mar-
bles takes it. They shake.)*

You live in the building?

(Marbles nods.)

You live here with your family? . . . You look like the family type. You gotta wife, I'll bet. Little boy, little girl.

(Marbles simply smokes.)

You know, they just found out that smoking cigarettes causes lung cancer. I just quit myself. Lucky's. LSMFT. Lucky Strike Makes Fine Tobacco . . . You employed?

(Marbles smokes.)

I didn't catch your name—what's your name? . . . Heck, it doesn't matter anyway, what matters is that your family's taken care of. Especially these days. These are uncertain times. And what a man needs for him and his family is security. With the death of Stalin and the Russians building all those missiles, who knows what's gonna happen to our future. If one of those babies hits, we Americans may be faced with some serious problems. And that's why there's no better time to purchase an insurance policy from Metropolitan Life. If something were to happen to you—say you're walking out the door to go buy a newspaper—and zap, you're vaporized by an A-bomb—what's your family gonna do? They'll be up shit's creek without a paddle—excuse my French but allow me to continue.

(Marbles engages a whoopee cushion hidden under his arm, pulls it out, plays with it lazily.)

A whoopee cushion! Hey that's great!

(Marbles tosses the whoopee cushion over his shoulder. From his vest pocket, Richard produces a brochure and hands it to Marbles.)

That brochure there breaks it all down for you. The premium payment for our new policies is quite low. Check those numbers out. Those numbers do not lie, friend—

(Marbles has balled the brochure up, popped it into his mouth and started to chew.)

You're eating it . . . I'll bet it's delicious.

(Marbles burps out the pulpy mass, catches it, tosses it over his shoulder.)

Look I don't blame you. What a bunch of crap, right? You try knocking on doors and doing that seven days a week, ten sometimes twelve hours a day. After a while the sound of your own voice just becomes repulsive. Like some awful clarinet hitting all the wrong notes.

The truth is I'm looking for my wife. Her name is Roselyn. Roselyn Bumper. Sometimes she tells people her name is Rose because, well, because she thinks it's her stage name . . . Rose Hathaway. I have a sneaking suspicion that she tried to come here today. Well, it's more than a sneaking suspicion, because I actually read about it in her journal. Probably not the most trustworthy thing a husband can do, but I felt I had the right, and I'll explain. You see, my wife is an actress, and last year she came very close to landing a role in a revival of this big fancy play on Broadway, but she didn't get it and she got very blue, really down in the dumps. She wouldn't get out of bed sometimes. And if she would, she would just stare off into space. In the middle of the night she walked into our neighbor's house and started to . . . well, let's just say some very embarrassing things happened. Things got so bad that I took her to be psychologically examined. She took all sorts of tests. This one doctor from the National Institute of Mental Health even suggested that she try floating in a sensory deprivation chamber. She would have to float for hours on end in a large vat of saltwater. Like some awful paralyzed sea creature. The bottom line is she really hasn't been well and I thought I could help in some small way. So what I did was I forged a letter from the playwright. He was at the audition you see. According to my wife he even shook her hand. The letter I wrote to her was very flattering and it really made her feel better. It really did make a world of difference for a while. And last night he died and I read in her journal that she believed he was still alive—that he'd set the whole thing up and faked his own death. So she decided that she would come find him here.

To thank him I guess, I don't know. And the reason she came here is because I looked in the phone book and found a Eugene O'Neill living at this very address. He's the playwright, you see, the one who she thought wrote her the letter. Well, to make a long story short, she disappeared today. We live in Connecticut—in Darien—and when I came back from my door-to-doors this afternoon she was gone. I normally wouldn't work on a Saturday, but things have been really stiff lately. Really hard-up.

(Back at the piano bench now, dejected.)

They've been . . . Well. Let's just say they've been hard. We're expecting our first child. We just found out a few weeks ago, so . . .

(Marbles leaps over the stairwell railing, approaches Bumper, fakes tripping just as he passes him, tumbles, then sits on the radiator.)

You're a performer, too!

(From the briefcase Richard produces a copy of Rose's headshot. He crosses to Marbles, picks up his cap for him, then

offers it in some failed attempt at performance. He offers
Marbles the headshot. Marbles accepts it.)

That's her there. She's beautiful, right? I wanted to give
her something. She was so heartbroken. They said she was
suffering from depressive tendencies—acute melancholia,
I guess they call it—and they gave her a round of elec-
troshock treatments, which is not an easy thing for anyone to go through. She barely remembered how to tie her
shoes for a while. They suggested I have her committed, but
I refused, because I don't think she's crazy. She's just confused . . . Do you speak English?

(Marbles responds in a made-up language. He speaks for a
long time. It might sound like French and Italian and Czech
and like something altogether ridiculous. His reply eventu-
ally comes to an end. Stunned, Richard crosses back to the
piano bench and sits.)

You have no idea what I just said, do you?

(Marbles rises off the cold radiator, crosses to the piano, sets
the headshot on the top, then removes the envelope from his
back pocket, hands it to Richard, crosses the length of the
hallway, all the way to the stairwell windows, climbs out of
one, closes it behind him, and ascends the fire escape.
  Richard Bumper opens the envelope and starts to read the
letter as the lights fade.)

END

PARAFFIN

CHARACTERS

DENNY KELLEN, thirty

MARGO KELLEN, Denny's wife, pregnant, thirty

LUCAS KELLEN, Denny's younger brother, late twenties

MARTY KUBIAK, sixties

KEVIN O'NEILL, the super, mid-thirties

RAHEL LEVY, Israeli woman, late twenties

IDO LEVY, Rahel's husband, Israeli, thirty

LESHIK, polish, late twenties

DENA PASZEK, Margo's friend, thirty

CORY, young friend of Marty's, African American

SETTING

A third-floor hallway of a pre-war tenement apartment building on the Lower East Side of Manhattan, 2003.

The third-floor hallway in a tenement on the Lower East Side.
Three apartments span the upstage wall. A stairwell right, with
a window. An apartment extreme stage left. Pushed against the
wall is an old upright piano. A piano bench on top of it. The hall
is illuminated by an overhead fluorescent light.

A beautiful summer day, August 14, 2003. Ten A.M.

Denny, thin, thirty, is lying on his stomach, unconscious in
the hallway. He wears skinny black jeans, no shirt, one two-tone,
vintage buckled leather shoe, no socks. He is pasty, filthy. His
hair is shaggy, unkempt. His fingernails are painted black. His
chest has been cut. One of his arms is twisted oddly behind his
back. It looks as if he's been thrown from a speeding car.

From the street, the sound of a car alarm. The sound of a
distant siren. A Spanish radio commercial dopplering by.

From an apartment, the sound of a morning TV show like
Regis and Kelly.

Marty Kubiak, an overweight man in his sixties, enters from
the stairwell. He is neat in appearance, wearing nice shorts and
a summer shirt, carrying a hatbox. He covers his nose, his mouth.
He sees Denny, approaches him, bends down, briefly assesses him,

*steps around him, knocks on a door. Moments later, Denny's wife,
Margo, thirty, opens the door. She is tired. She wears boxers, a
T-shirt. She is barefoot. She is six-and-a-half-months pregnant.*

MARGO: Hi, Marty. What's up?
MARTY: Your husband's in the hall again.

(Margo looks into the hall, sees Denny, crosses to him.)

He doesn't appear to be conscious. Should I call an ambu-
lance?
MARGO: I'll take care of it. What's that smell?
MARTY: I think he might have done a number two.
MARGO: Jesus, Denny. Sorry, Marty.
MARTY: It's obviously not your fault.

*(Margo exits into her apartment, returns with a cylinder of
air freshener, sprays the seat of Denny's pants.)*

If you need anything, don't hesitate to knock on my door.

(Marty keys into his apartment, closes the door.)

MARGO *(To Denny)*: Denny, Get up.

(No response. She prods him again.)

Denny . . . Get up, Denny.

*(Still no response. She exits into her apartment with the cyl-
inder of air freshener, leaving the door open, returns with a
pitcher of water, douses him. He wakes with a start, quickly
curls into a ball, terrified, hands clasped over his head, crash
position, as if he is about to be beaten.)*

Denny, it's me . . . Denny!

(He looks up, disoriented.)

It's almost 10:30. Aren't you supposed to meet the truck?
DENNY: Jesus, the truck. The fucking truck! Fuck!

(He pushes himself up off the floor, manages to sit.)

MARGO: Rough night?
DENNY: Pretty rough, yeah.
MARGO: Where'd you go after the gig?
DENNY: Out.
MARGO: Out meaning where?
DENNY: Mars Bar. Niagara. The usual.
MARGO: Did Piano's pay you?
DENNY: Yeah.
MARGO: Good crowd?
DENNY: It was packed.
MARGO: What'd you guys make?
DENNY: Three hundred somethin'.
MARGO: Where's your cut?
DENNY: I don't have it.
MARGO: Why not?
DENNY: Because I don't. I owed this guy.
MARGO: What guy?
DENNY: This guy from the truck.
MARGO: Owed him for what?
DENNY: He helped us out with the rent a few months ago.
MARGO: What month?
DENNY: May. I mean June.
MARGO: May I mean June?
DENNY: June. It was definitely June. He's a good guy. Angus
  calls him in for museum jobs.
MARGO: How come I never knew about this?
DENNY: Because I didn't want to worry you.
MARGO: What's his name?
DENNY: Derek.

MARGO: Derek what?

DENNY: Fungo.

MARGO: Derek fucking Fungo?

DENNY: That's his name. He came to the gig. I paid him what I owed him.

MARGO: Why didn't you come home?

DENNY: I came home.

MARGO: Yeah, nine hours after you said you would.

DENNY: I got caught up.

MARGO: You got caught up.

DENNY: Kinda sorta, yeah.

MARGO: Caught up doing what?

DENNY: Nothing.

MARGO: I see you shit your pants again.

DENNY: Fuck! I shit my pants!

MARGO: Who were you with?

DENNY: Lloyd and Ellis.

MARGO: You guys got "caught up," huh?

DENNY: I came home eventually. I knocked on the door for like an hour.

MARGO: That's funny because I didn't hear it and I was up all night.

DENNY: Well, I don't know what to say—I knocked.

MARGO: You could've called. Where's your cell?

DENNY: The battery died.

MARGO: The battery died.

DENNY: Yeah, it died.

MARGO: Show it to me.

DENNY: The battery?

MARGO: The phone.

DENNY: Why?

MARGO: Because I want to see it.

DENNY: It died.

MARGO: Where is it, Denny?

DENNY: I don't have it, okay?

MARGO: You sold it.

DENNY: No I didn't, I left it at Niagara. It died and Ivan was charging it for me. It's prolly behind the bar.

(She moves to him, grabs his arm, he pulls it away.)

MARGO: Let me see your arm.

(He puts his left arm behind his back.)

Show me your arm, Denny.

(He doesn't budge.)

"Caught up," my ass.

(A hard silence.)

(Without pity) Where's your shirt, anyway?
DENNY: Fuck, my shirt. Fuck!
MARGO: Did you sell that, too?
DENNY: I didn't sell anything! What could I possibly get for that stupid shirt?!
MARGO: That stupid shirt was a Christmas present. It was Prada and it cost a helluva lot more than you think. And you're missing a shoe.
DENNY: Oh, fuck! My other Monte Carlo!! Jesus . . .

(He starts to cry.)

MARGO: Oh, now you're gonna cry? About your shoe?
DENNY *(Crying)*: I'm sorry, Margo. It was a bad night.
MARGO: I thought you said Piano's was packed.
DENNY: I'm talkin' about afterwards. Some crazy shit went down. It was a really, really bad night.
MARGO: . . . You about done crying?
DENNY: Yes.

MARGO: You know, you haven't asked me a single question?

DENNY: What am I supposed to ask you?

MARGO: You could start with: "How are you, Margo?" "How's your back?"

DENNY: How are you, Margo? How's your back?

MARGO: Fuck you.

DENNY: I'm really asking! How's your back? Seriously.

MARGO: Last night was agony. I got about forty-five minutes of sleep.

DENNY: That's prolly when I knocked . . . Did you use the heating pad?

MARGO: That thing just makes me hot.

DENNY: Well, then we should get that new mattress.

MARGO: And pay for it how?

DENNY: Fucking charge the thing.

MARGO: Denny, do you have any idea how much credit card debt we've amassed in the last six months? Between your new amp and the guitar and that stupid jacket.

DENNY: That jacket's not stupid.

MARGO: It's ridiculous. You hardly even wear it.

DENNY: It's my suicide jacket. I wear it.

MARGO: You put it on in front of the mirror and make faces. I don't think you've ever worn it out of the house . . . We're lucky I have insurance.

DENNY: . . . I'm sorry about your back . . . What'd you do last night?

MARGO: I watched a movie.

DENNY: With who, Dena?

MARGO: Your brother.

DENNY: You did? What movie?

MARGO: *The Shawshank Redemption.*

DENNY: That movie's corny.

MARGO: You're corny.

DENNY: Was Lucas being an asshole?

MARGO: No.

DENNY: Did he drink all my beer?

MARGO: I bought that beer.

DENNY: Yeah, but you can't drink it.

MARGO: I drink what I wanna drink.

DENNY: Pregnant chicks think they're so tough.

(Beat.)

If you let me in I'll give you a massage.

MARGO: No thanks.

DENNY: Why not?

MARGO: Because you're a filthy disgusting mess and I don't want you touching me.

DENNY: Can I at least take a shower?

MARGO: You're not coming in here, no. What happened to your chest, anyway?

DENNY: That was the crazy shit that went down.

MARGO: Uh-huh.

DENNY: Ellis got in a fight.

MARGO: With who?

DENNY: Lezcano.

MARGO: Who's Lezcano?

DENNY: Puerto Rican guy from Mount Vernon. He claimed Ellis owed him money and they had words. One thing led to another.

MARGO: Looks to me like you're the one who got in the fight.

DENNY: I was trying to break it up and Lezcano cut me.

MARGO: With what.

DENNY: A comb.

MARGO: He cut you with a fucking comb?

DENNY: Yeah. He combed me.

MARGO: Was it like a switchblade comb?

DENNY: It was an unbreakable comb.

MARGO: Did you clean it?

DENNY: The comb?

MARGO: The wound.

DENNY: Of course.

MARGO: No you didn't.

DENNY: It's not even that deep.

MARGO: Where's your guitar?

DENNY: Lloyd has it.

MARGO: Why does Lloyd have it?

DENNY: Because he does.

MARGO: Denny, if you sold that guitar!

DENNY: I didn't sell it, Margo! Lloyd's gonna fix one of the pick-ups! I'm getting it back tomorrow! Jesus, are you my wife or a fucking cop?!

(He starts to cough convulsively, can't quite get himself to stop, eventually he does stop.)

MARGO: You're lucky I'm not a cop.

DENNY: Look, I'm sorry. Okay? I'm hugely sorry. I'm an avalanche of regret and sorrow. Can I please come in?

(The phone rings. Margo enters the apartment. Denny tries to follow her inside but she closes the door in his face, locking it. He searches for his keys, looks in all pockets, in his wallet. No luck.

Kevin O'Neill, the super, enters from the apartment at the other end of the hall. He wears a Yankees T-shirt and old maintenance man pants. He is mid-thirties, a bit doughy, perhaps balding, seems older than he is.)

KEVIN: Everything okay, Mr. Kellen?

DENNY: Everything's fine.

KEVIN: You locked out?

DENNY: Not really. Margo's in there.

KEVIN: I'd prefer it if you didn't fight in the hall.

DENNY: I know. Me, too. Sorry.

KEVIN *(Referring to his chest)*: Did she do that?

DENNY: Yeah, in the scuffle. It's just a little cut.

KEVIN: Did she try stabbin' you or somethin'?

DENNY: No, it's from this swan statue that her mom gave us when we got married. This crystal swan. She threw it at me. It's pretty sharp. The feathers.

KEVIN: Is Margo okay?

DENNY: She's fine. She's just in there calming down. It's been a bit of a rollercoaster lately. Being pregnant. The hormones, you know?

KEVIN: Hormones, sure.

DENNY: We started couple's therapy the other day. With like a shrink.

KEVIN: That's really none of my business.

DENNY: I totally agree with you, Kevin. Totally agree.

KEVIN: You mind me askin' a personal question?

DENNY: Not at all. What?

KEVIN: Did you shit your pants or something? Because it smells like someone shit their pants out here . . . You might want to check . . . By the way, I'm sure it's not exactly what you wanted to hear about right now, but Management called again.

DENNY: I put the rent in the mail yesterday.

KEVIN: That's what you said last month.

DENNY: I did, Kevin, I really did.

KEVIN: Mr. Yamagushi hasn't received it.

DENNY: Kevin, do me a favor and tell Mr. Yamagushi it's on its way . . . I've been making good money lately. My band just got signed to Astralwerks, so . . .

KEVIN: You don't gotta explain it to me.

DENNY: I'm just sayin'. In case Mr. Yamagushi asks.

KEVIN: Do me a favor and get cleaned up, huh? I got mice in unit six, rats in the basement, and now you're shittin' your friggin' pants in my hallway?

(Kevin enters his apartment, closes the door.

Denny knocks on his own door. Nothing. He touches the cut on his chest, knocks again. Margo opens the door. She is holding a clean T-shirt, work boots, pants, underwear, socks, hands them to him.)

DENNY: Who was on the phone?

MARGO: Angus. They're in Long Island City. 4113 Queens Boulevard. The truck is parked in front of some sushi restaurant. I told him you slept through your alarm and that you were on your way.

DENNY: Fucking Long Island City?

MARGO: It's the 7 Train.

(She proffers a damp towel.)

(Referring to his soiled clothes) Give me those.

(He removes his pants and underwear. He takes the towel, cleans himself. He steps into the fresh underwear, pants, socks. Puts on the T-shirt, hands the towel back, gives her his soiled clothes, his one shoe, takes the boots. She hands him a tube of ointment.)

DENNY: What's this?

MARGO: It'll keep that from getting infected.

(Denny takes it.)

DENNY: Fucking Lozano.

MARGO: Lozano or Lezcano?

DENNY: I mean Lezcano. Lozano's this other guy. Italian guy from Bay Ridge.

MARGO: Right.

DENNY: Does sound at Trash Bar.

MARGO: Lezcano's the Puerto Rican.

DENNY: The Puerto Rican from Mount Vernon, yeah.

MARGO: The guy who combed you.

(He touches the wound on his chest, applies some ointment.)

So you better get going.

DENNY: Can I at least have a hug?

(She steps toward him. They hug.)

You smell good . . .

MARGO: Denny . . .

DENNY: You always smell so good.

MARGO: And you stink.

(He starts to kiss her neck.)

Denny, don't.

(She relents a bit. He smells her hair, inhales deeply.)

Stop.

(He doesn't. She pushes him away.)

DENNY: I thought of another name: Olive.

MARGO: Olive what?

DENNY: Olive Marie. It's pretty, right? . . . Hopefully she'll get your looks. Pretty Olive Marie Kellen. I've been thinking about her a lot lately. I've been thinking about everything, I really have.

MARGO: Go to work, Denny.

DENNY: Can I borrow your MetroCard?

MARGO: I put it in your pant's pocket.

DENNY: Thanks. What are you gonna do today?

MARGO: I don't know. I might go to a movie with Dena.

DENNY: Isn't Dena working?

MARGO: She works from home on Thursdays.

DENNY: What movie?

MARGO: Maybe *S.W.A.T.*

DENNY: Who's in that?

MARGO: Colin Farrell.

DENNY: You think he's good?

MARGO: I do, yeah.

DENNY: English pretty boy.

MARGO: He's actually Irish. And he's more bad boy than pretty boy.

DENNY: More bad boy, huh? You think he's handsome?

MARGO: He's handsome.

DENNY: On a scale of one to ten.

MARGO: Eight, maybe nine.

DENNY: Guys that short can't be nines.

MARGO: Is he short?

DENNY: He's short and he's a total cokehead. I've seen him at Niagara with that other shmacktor. The one with the birthmark who lives above Two Boots. Total cokeheads.

MARGO: And who the fuck are you to judge?

DENNY: You always look so pretty in the morning.

(He takes a step toward her. She takes a step back.)

I really want to sleep in our bed tonight.

MARGO: You know what we've agreed upon.

DENNY: Yeah, yeah, yeah. The agreement . . . I love you, Margo.

MARGO: You need help.

DENNY: I need you to be there for me is what I need.

MARGO: Come home high and I'm changing the locks.

(She shuts the door. Denny presses his ear to it, listens, then quietly turns the knob. From the other side the deadbolt turns. He crosses to the end of the hallway, ascends the stairwell, creeping. From somewhere in the building, the sound of rock music. A TV show from Kevin's apartment. A fire truck from the street. Margo enters the hallway, fully dressed now, and exits down the stairs. Denny appears in the stairwell, waits till he hears the front door to the building close, crosses to Kevin's door, knocks. Kevin answers, the TV on in the background.)

DENNY: Hey, can you let me into my apartment? I forgot my wallet and my keys.

KEVIN: Where's Margo?

DENNY: She just left.

KEVIN: Where'd she go?

DENNY: She had to go see our obstetrician.

(Kevin stares at him.)

Come on, bro, I'm late for work.

(Kevin stares at him.)

I'm sorta desperate here, Kevin.

(Kevin exits into his apartment, returns with a set of many keys, works Denny's key off the chain, hands it to him.)

You're a lifesaver.

KEVIN: Leave it under the mat.

(Kevin crosses to his apartment, enters, closes the door.
From the apartment across the hall, Lucas, Denny's younger brother, enters in a wheelchair. He is late twenties, dressed in sweatpants and a T-shirt, a necklace of dogtags under his shirt. His hair is a bit unwieldy and he hasn't shaved, though he is handsome. He wheels over to the Kellens' door, presses his ear to it, listens. Denny opens the door, holding the aforementioned crystal swan and three or four silk dresses. He is also wearing his suicide jacket, which is a thin, vintage Italian leather jacket with a noose sewn into the collar and down the back. Lucas is parked in front of the door, blocking the way.)

DENNY: Lucas. Jesus you scared me.

LUCAS: Where are you going?

DENNY: To work.

LUCAS: How'd you get in?

DENNY: With a key.

LUCAS: Whose key?

DENNY: My key.

LUCAS: Yeah?

DENNY: Yeah.

LUCAS: You sure about that?

DENNY: Pretty sure, yeah.

LUCAS: Your key.

DENNY: Yes!

LUCAS: Where's Margo?

DENNY: She went out.

LUCAS: Out where?

DENNY: Just out. What the fuck business is it of yours, anyway?

LUCAS: You don't think it's my business?

DENNY: Can you please move? I'm sort of in a hurry.

LUCAS (*Referring to the swan*): What are you doing with that?

DENNY: I'm taking it to get polished.

LUCAS: Why?

DENNY: Why? Because Margo's mom is coming into town for Labor Day weekend. When she comes into town we polish the swan.

LUCAS: And the dresses?

DENNY: I'm dropping them off at the dry cleaners. Can you please move?

LUCAS: This guy came around looking for you.

DENNY: What guy?

LUCAS: Just this guy.

DENNY: What'd he look like?

LUCAS: Tall. Big head. Face like a catfish.

DENNY: Dominican guy?

LUCAS: White guy. Maybe Polish or Russian.

DENNY: When?

LUCAS: The other day?

DENNY: Like yesterday?

LUCAS: Maybe, yeah. He knocked on your door for like ten minutes. I came out into the hallway because he wouldn't stop.

DENNY: Well, he was obviously looking for the wrong person.

LUCAS: No, he seemed pretty certain of who he was looking for. He used your name.

DENNY: Like my first name?

LUCAS: He said, "Does Denny Kellen live here?"

DENNY: What'd you tell him?

LUCAS: I told him you did.

DENNY: Great. Thanks, Lucas. My only brother lookin' out for me as usual.

LUCAS: He told me to tell you that he's the guy with the machete. It all felt pretty ominous.

DENNY: Jesus.

LUCAS: Speaking of Jesus, Mom wants you to call her.

DENNY: Shit. Fucking Mom. How's her hip?

LUCAS: Her hip is fine. I think she somehow knows things aren't so good between you and Margo.

DENNY: I s'pose you told her that too.

LUCAS: Don't worry, she said she's praying for you guys.

DENNY: Anything else?

LUCAS: Yeah, this.

(Lucas quickly grabs Denny's arm. There is a brief struggle. Despite the wheelchair, Lucas manages to get him in a hold that is very painful, brings Denny to his knees. Lucas sees the track marks.)

(Seething, hateful) Do you have any self-respect?!

(Lucas digs in.)

DO YOU?!!

(Denny cries out. Marty comes into the hallway. Lucas releases Denny's arm.)

MARTY: Everything okay out here?

DENNY *(Catching his breath, holding his arm)*: I gotta go meet the truck, Lucas.

(Lucas reverses, moves out of the way. Denny closes the door, locks it. Denny heads for the stairwell when Kevin opens the door, holding his hand out for the spare key. Denny hands it to him, exits down the stairs.)

KEVIN: You're welcome.

(Kevin reenters his apartment, closes the door.)

MARTY: Lucas.

LUCAS: What.

MARTY: You know what.

LUCAS: He's a fucking junky scumbag.

MARTY: He needs your sympathy.

LUCAS: He doesn't deserve it.

MARTY: I'm sure you could find it in your heart. Especially after everything you've been through.

LUCAS: He's an embarrassment.

MARTY: I wonder what your parents would think if they heard you say that?

LUCAS: What do you know about my parents?

MARTY: I know your father pays me a thousand dollars a month because he wanted you to have the opportunity to experience New York City, which according to his last letter was something you've wanted to do since you were in high school. And I also know your mother is happy that her two boys are together so they can look out for each other this summer. I actually have that saved on my answering machine if you'd like to listen to it.

LUCAS: Can't you go somewhere? Like to a day spa? Or Canada?

MARTY: I've lived in this apartment for thirty-two years, Lucas. I think I've earned the right to come and go as I please.

LUCAS: Why don't you go over to West 4th Street and find your-self a homo thug. Raheem or Dooji. If you take him to Foot Locker and buy him a new pair of kicks I'll bet you can get him to do just about anything.

MARTY: What the hell do you know about homo thugs?

LUCAS: I've seen your porn collection. And your *ESPN The Magazine* subscription. And your MTV Streetball DVDs. You should get a job coaching basketball at the Boys' Club. You'd be in pervert Heaven.

MARTY: Lucas, do you actually hear the things you say to the people who care about you? It's astonishing.

LUCAS: Marty, I'm renting a room in your apartment. We are not family. And despite what my dad may write on a scrap of paper thrown in with the rent check or what my pathetic mother might whine about on your mid-eighties, analog, blue-light-special answering machine, we are most cer-tainly not friends.

MARTY: I'm sorry you feel that way.

LUCAS: Save your sorrow for yourself.

MARTY: Lucas, you'll have to forgive me if this comes off as half-baked wisdom from an old queen whom you undoubtedly detest, but I happen to think there's still some good in you. Despite your bitterness, despite your capacity for small-ness and cruelty, whether you like it or not, there's still something alive in that faulty body of yours, and I'd bet my favorite hat that it's your heart. But until you start living your life like you possess that vital muscle, you're going to be stuck in a dark place for a very long time.

LUCAS: Get a life.

MARTY: I've been trying to get a life for going on forty-five years. Believe me, I'm doing my best.

(Marty goes back inside, shuts the door. Lucas wheels down to the piano. He stares at the keys for a moment and then starts hammering away at them, pounding with his fists.

Kevin enters the hallway, glaring at Lucas. Lucas ceases the pounding, mockingly lowers the lid.)

LUCAS *(Smartass)*: Hi, tubby.

(Kevin says nothing.)

You sure look nice today in your smart-fitting trousers and designer T-shirt. Hey, by the way, I think there's a crocodile in Marty Kubiak's toilet and it's really screwing with my rectal well-being, can you take a look at it?

KEVIN *(Exiting into his apartment)*: Douchebag.

(Kevin closes the door. Lucas lifts the lid of the piano, considers pounding on it, instead he starts to play. It's something quite beautiful, Brahms perhaps. Rahel, an Israeli woman, late twenties, ascends the stairwell, holding a bag from the market. Lucas senses that he is being watched, and stops playing.)

RAHEL: That was beautiful.

(He says nothing.)

I some day wish to learn.

LUCAS: It's an overrated instrument. Ultimately it just makes you feel lonely.

RAHEL: You play all your life?

LUCAS: I had one in my house growing up. Took lessons as a kid. I wound up hating it like most people who take lessons as a kid. What's in the bag?

RAHEL: Fennel.

LUCAS: Every time I see you you have vegetables.

RAHEL: Fennel is not vegetable.

LUCAS: What is it?

RAHEL: It is *(Mispronounces with hard H)* herb.

LUCAS *(Mocking her mispronunciation)*: It's a *herb*?

RAHEL: Yes.

LUCAS: What's it for?

RAHEL: Salad.

LUCAS: What's your name again?

RAHEL: Ra*h*el.

LUCAS *(Really hitting the H's)*: You toss a lot of herbal salads, Rahel?

RAHEL: Sometimes.

LUCAS: You're the occasional salad tosser? What's it like outside?

RAHEL: It's a beautiful day.

LUCAS: Birds, babies, puppies, cloudless sky?

RAHEL: There are very few clouds.

LUCAS: It's Thursday, right?

RAHEL: I think so, yes.

LUCAS: For obvious reasons I can't get up and down the stairs too well, so the deprivation of sunlight can make time flatten out.

RAHEL: What is "flatten out"?

LUCAS: Flatten out. Lose its shape.

(Beat.)

RAHEL: You are always in this hallway. Every time I pass.

LUCAS: Pathetic, right? Like Time, I'm losing my shape.

RAHEL: You are flattening out.

LUCAS: Yes, especially my once Nubian ass.

RAHEL: How long have you been in the wheelchair?

LUCAS: Going on eight months.

RAHEL: Were you in a car accident?

LUCAS: Yeah, a big international car accident called Afghanistan.

RAHEL: You were soldier?

LUCAS: Yep. I got shot looking for the big bad wolf.

RAHEL: Who is this?

LUCAS *(An exaggerated big whisper)*: Osama.

RAHEL: Sorry.

LUCAS: Don't be sorry, it's only partly your fault. Just kidding.

RAHEL: They will never find him.

LUCAS: How can you be so sure?

RAHEL: It is like hunting leopard in the jungle. You can never catch because it becomes the tree, the water, other animals.

LUCAS: How metaphysical. I think our man's a little tall to be a leopard.

RAHEL: But the trees are also tall.

LUCAS: We're actually talking about an intricate subterranean Afghani cave system here, but by all means, please continue with the fable-like jungle imagery.

RAHEL: If you don't know the jungle, the animals can keep changing their shapes.

LUCAS: But if you burn the jungle down all the animals have to eventually come out. The elephants, the giraffes, the spider monkeys, even the leopards.

RAHEL: But perhaps the leopard becomes the fire, and then what?

LUCAS: Then we fly in a shitload of hibachis and have us a big ol' Middle-Eastern barbecue! Pass the fucking shwarma! . . . You think our country is stupid.

RAHEL: I like this country.

LUCAS: What do you like about it?

RAHEL: Many things.

LUCAS: Name one.

RAHEL: Dean and Deluca.

LUCAS: Is that where you get your fennel?

RAHEL: No. I only go there to look.

LUCAS: Where are you from, anyway?

RAHEL: Israel.

LUCAS: Now there's a mess.

RAHEL: I was in the army, too.

LUCAS: Oh, yeah?

RAHEL: For two years. In Israel it is required.

LUCAS: So what does that mean, you can do a hundred push-ups? You can find your way through your local obstacle course?

. . . You know, I saw you earlier. I was watching you from my bedroom window. You were walking away from the building. You kept wiping your face with the back of your hand.

RAHEL: You spy.

LUCAS: I'm just looking out my window. What were you so upset about?

RAHEL: None of your business.

LUCAS: In my book if you're crying and I'm watching you it's my business.

RAHEL: Life is difficult.

LUCAS: How so?

RAHEL: My husband.

LUCAS: Marriage, colon. "Why do it?" he asks.

RAHEL: You are married?

LUCAS: To my hand, but that's none of your business. Hey, what's your husband's name again?

RAHEL: Ido.

LUCAS: Ido, right. Is Ido a bad husband?

RAHEL: No.

LUCAS: Are you a bad wife?

RAHEL: No.

LUCAS: Then what's the problem? Not enough cream in your coffee?

RAHEL: He is gone so much.

LUCAS: Ah, the old nothing-to-do-while-Dodo's-away syndrome.

RAHEL: Ido.

LUCAS: Ido, right. Is Ido home now?

RAHEL: He is in New Jersey.

LUCAS: What's Ido doing in New Jersey?

RAHEL: Buying fabric.

LUCAS: For what?

RAHEL: His job.

LUCAS: Does Ido buy a lot of fabric?

RAHEL: He is design consultant.

LUCAS: How crushingly masculine . . . So you were crying because you miss him. How sweet.

RAHEL: Sometimes I wish things were different.

LUCAS: Things meaning . . .

RAHEL: My life.

LUCAS: Different in what way?

RAHEL: Just different. Do you ever feel that way? Like you could just start walking some place?

(He doesn't answer. A beat.)

LUCAS: Will Ido be gone all day?

RAHEL: He'll be back this afternoon.

LUCAS: Want to come over later?

RAHEL: And do what?

LUCAS: I don't know. Play checkers. Watch a movie. Thumb wrestle.

RAHEL: What is thumb wrestle?

LUCAS: You know what your thumbs are?

RAHEL: Of course.

LUCAS: And do you know what wrestling is?

RAHEL: No.

LUCAS: It's a sport where men grapple.

RAHEL: What is grapple?

LUCAS: Grab hold of. In wrestling, you grapple until your opponent can no longer move. And it often involves mounting. As in one man mounts the other one until he is pinned. So thumb wrestling is . . . well, you do the math.

(Rahel is clearly confused.)

I'll pay you a hundred bucks.

RAHEL: Pay?

LUCAS: One hundred grade-A U.S. dollars.

RAHEL: Pay for what?

LUCAS: To watch a movie with me? Or to grapple? Or to let me delicately pin you? You can tell Dig-Dug I'm giving you piano lessons.

RAHEL: Ido.

(Margo enters with groceries. Rahel quickly exits.)

LUCAS *(To Rahel, up the stairs)*: Or we could just thumb wrestle.

(Margo crosses to her door. Lucas wheels down the hall after her. Just as she gets her keys out:)

I'll kill him if you want me to.

MARGO: You'll kill him, huh?

(She gets her apartment key out.)

LUCAS: I'm serious. I have a gun. Nine-millimeter Glock. Wanna see it?

MARGO: Not particularly.

LUCAS: You afraid of guns?

MARGO: No.

LUCAS: He's a junky scumbag.

MARGO: He's still my husband. And not to mention your brother.

(She enters her apartment, closes the door.
Marty enters the hallway, closes his door, starts down the hall.)

LUCAS: Where are you going?

MARTY: To Canada, I'll send you a postcard.

(Lucas reaches into his pocket, produces a cell phone.)

LUCAS: Here, take my cell.

MARTY: Why?

LUCAS: I don't know. Just in case.

MARTY: Just in case what—I fall into a homophobic pothole? Wouldn't that make you happy?

LUCAS: Just take it, Marty.

MARTY: Don't worry, I'll be sure to drink plenty of fluids.

LUCAS: Do you have your insulin?

(Margo opens her door.)

MARGO: Marty, my mom is coming into town for Labor Day weekend and I'd love to give her one of your hats.

MARTY: Great.

LUCAS: Marty.

MARTY: What, Lucas?

LUCAS: DO YOU HAVE YOUR INSULIN?

MARTY: Of course I have my insulin. *(To Margo)* Did you have one in mind?

MARGO: I think she'd really like that one you were showing me the other day.

MARTY: You mean the kelly green one with the side gather?

MARGO: The one with the little bow, yeah.

MARTY: Would you happen to know her head size?

MARGO: I think she's a seven but I'll confirm that and let you know.

MARTY: I certainly do appreciate the business.

LUCAS: Are you sure you have it?

MARTY: Yes I'm sure, Lucas! I always have my damn insulin! I've been a fucking diabetic for over thirty years! I don't have Alzheimer's!

(Marty exits down the stairwell. Lucas wheels after him.)

LUCAS: Will you at least call later? . . . Marty!

(The sound of the apartment building door closing. Lucas wheels back.)

He shouldn't be going out in that heat.

MARGO: You've gotten attached.

LUCAS: Hardly.

MARGO: No, it's sweet.

LUCAS: Sharing a toilet with the Village People's version of Homer Simpson isn't exactly what I would call sweet.

MARGO: Hey, you really shouldn't complain. You got what you wanted: you're in New York for the summer. You have your own air-conditioned room, free wireless internet, a fully stocked fridge—

LUCAS: And my very own enormous gay roommate.

MARGO: Homophobe.

LUCAS: You're damn right.

(Margo produces a joint.)

MARGO: Want some?

LUCAS: No. I mean fuck yes.

(She lights the joint, smokes it, passes to him, he smokes, passes back. She eases down the wall, sits. They smoke over the following:)

MARGO: So why do you own a gun?

LUCAS: Because I do.

(They smoke.)

Why do you smoke pot when you're six-and-a-half months pregnant?

MARGO: Because I do.

LUCAS: You want my nephew-slash-niece to be born with extra toes? Or a fin?

MARGO: She'd be my little fish baby.

LUCAS: She? I thought you didn't know.

MARGO: I found out last week.

LUCAS: Thanks for telling me. Does Denny know?

(She nods.)

He's always wanted a girl. He'll probably ruin her life.
MARGO: Knock it off.

(They smoke.)

LUCAS: So have you officially kicked him out?
MARGO: I only let him in under certain conditions.
LUCAS: Which means what, he gets to use the bathroom if he
    writes "I've been a very bad man" in his dream journal five
    hundred times? Have you changed the locks yet?

(She doesn't answer.)

I can't fucking believe you haven't changed the locks.
MARGO: Lucas, just smoke my pot and be nice.

(Kevin opens his door, holding a book.)

KEVIN: I got friggin' mosquitoes nesting in my air conditioner.
    I'll prolly get West Nile or Hepatitis or some shit.
MARGO: Hi, Kevin.
KEVIN: Hey, Margo.
LUCAS: Hi, Sweet Tits.
KEVIN: Margo, you gonna see your friend Dena anytime soon?
MARGO: I'm seeing her later today, why?
KEVIN *(Offering the book)*: Could you do me a favor and give
    this to her?
MARGO *(Reading the title)*: *Harry Potter and the Prisoner of
    Azkaban.*
KEVIN: I just finished *Goblet of Fire*, but that one's by far my
    favorite. Don't get me wrong—they're all great. But the
    whole traitor theme in *Azkaban* is just awesome. It's a
    signed first edition, too, so . . .
MARGO: It's signed. Wow. *(Reading from the title page)* To Kevin.
    Best wishes, J. K. Rowling.

KEVIN: Yeah, I caught her at the Barnes & Noble at Union Square a coupla months ago. You shoulda seen the line. Like the Beatles at Shea.

LUCAS: The Beatles at Shea? What are you, like sixty?

MARGO: I'm sure she'll take good care of it.

KEVIN: Last time I saw her we got to talkin' and she told me how she loved *Potter*, so . . . By the way, does she got a boyfriend?

LUCAS: Yeah, me. Wanna smell my finger?

KEVIN: If you haven't noticed, I'm ignoring you, fucko.

MARGO: I'm pretty sure she's single.

LUCAS: Before you fully pursue this you really should smell my finger.

KEVIN: What does she do?

MARGO: She works in book publishing.

LUCAS: She edits a series of coffee table books chronicling the world's most horrific venereal disasters.

MARGO: She's a junior fiction editor at Viking.

KEVIN: Well, I love books. Fiction, nonfiction, true crime, whatever.

MARGO: I'll be sure she gets this.

KEVIN: Thanks. *(To both)* Hey, and do me a solid and don't smoke too much of that stuff out here. I could care less about what you do in the privacy of your own home, but not in my hallway, huh?

LUCAS: *Your* hallway?

KEVIN: You know what I mean.

LUCAS: No, I don't actually. Did Mr. Yamagushi sell you the building?

MARGO: It's my fault. Sorry, Kevin. *(She stubs out the joint)*

(Kevin exits into his apartment.)

(Holding up the book) Looks like Dena started a book club.

(She waves the smoke toward the open window.)

LUCAS: How's your back?

MARGO: It aches. The pot helps me fall asleep, but I keep waking up in the middle of the night. I wish you'd give me a painkiller.

LUCAS: You wanna take my oxycotton away from me?

MARGO: Just one.

LUCAS: What about *my* pain?

MARGO: Please, Lucas? I need a good night's sleep.

LUCAS: You sound like Denny. *(Producing a multiday container of pills)* This can't be good for my future niece.

(He undoes the bottle of pills, hands her one.)

MARGO: Hey.

LUCAS: Hey what.

MARGO: Show me your gun.

(They watch each other as the lights fade.)

3:30 P.M.

Kevin enters the hallway from his apartment, carrying an air conditioner. He exits with it down the stairs, leaving his door open. Marty's door opens and Lucas quickly wheels himself over to Kevin's apartment, and enters it. The hallway is dead for a moment. Then Lucas emerges with a case of beer in his lap. He quickly lets himself into Marty's apartment, and closes the door.

Kevin can be heard ascending the stairs. He enters the hallway, exits into his apartment.

Leshik, a Polish man in his late twenties, enters the hallway, ascending the stairwell. He wears a track suit and carries something wrapped in a dishtowel, something approximately the size of a volleyball. He crosses to Margo and Denny's apartment, knocks on the door.

Dena, Margo's friend, answers the door. She is thirty, bookish. She wears glasses.

LESHIK: Hello.
DENA: Hello.
LESHIK: Is Denny Kellen home?

DENA: No.

LESHIK: Is Margo Kellen home?

DENA: She's in the shower.

LESHIK: She is the wife of Denny Kellen, no?

DENA: Who are you exactly?

LESHIK: My name is Leshik. You are?

DENA: Dena.

LESHIK: Dena. Do you have last name?

DENA: Paszek.

LESHIK *(Excited)*: Paszek?

DENA: Yeah, Paszek.

LESHIK: How you spell?

DENA: Um, P-a-s-z-e-k.

LESHIK: This is Polish name!

DENA: I'm half Polish.

LESHIK: Your mother?

DENA: My father.

LESHIK: I am Polish, too! I am from Warsaw!

DENA: I'm from Kalamazoo.

LESHIK *(Offering his hand)*: Pleased to meet you, Dena Paszek!

DENA: Nice to meet you, too.

(They shake.)

LESHIK: Leshik.

DENA: Leshik.

LESHIK: You are Margo Kellen's lesbian lover.

DENA: Um, we're just friends.

LESHIK: You also live here?

DENA: I'm just visiting.

LESHIK: Very good . . . What is your other half?

DENA: I don't understand your question.

LESHIK: Your mother is not Polish.

DENA: Oh, I'm half Korean. I'm sort of a mutt.

LESHIK: You are dog?

DENA: My mother's Korean and my father's mostly Polish.

LESHIK: Because your mother's family have many orgies.

DENA: I'm not so sure about that. I'll have to ask.

LESHIK: Do you know when Denny Kellen will be home?

DENA: I'm afraid I don't. But I'd be happy to pass along a message to Margo.

LESHIK: Yes, okay, good.

(He removes the dishtowel to reveal the crystal swan that Denny had exited with a few hours earlier.)

Please tell to Margo Kellen that Denny Kellen try to give this to Balboa but Balboa does not want stupid glass chicken from Ikea.

(He hands her the swan.)

DENA: Um, this is a swan. I believe it's actually a wedding gift and I highly doubt that it's from Ikea. I'm almost certain that it's fine crystal and most likely worth a lot of money.

LESHIK: It is wedding gift?

(Dena nods.)

Denny Kellen try to give Balboa wedding gift?

DENA: I guess he did, yeah.

LESHIK: What kind of man is this?

DENA: Good question.

LESHIK: Margo Kellen is married to this person? He is shit in toilet bowel.

DENA: I'm not entirely disagreeing with you.

LESHIK: He has no balls. They are nothing, these balls. Balboa does not want wedding gift.

(He says something to himself in Polish, disgusted with Denny's character, then gathers himself.)

Excuse me, I am truly disgusted.

DENA: No problem.

LESHIK: Dena Paszek, I continue message, thank you. Please also tell to Margo Kellen to tell to Denny Kellen that if he does not meet Balboa at disgust location at disgust time with disgust amount of money that he will be hunted like wild boar and stabbed many times with screwdriver and then Balboa and his rottweiler-style dog Larry Johnson will fuck him in these holes with their penis erections along with my rottweiler-style dog Dudu and my cornsnake Sasha and ferret belonging to fat black gangster called Booker T With Remedy.

DENA: That's some message.

LESHIK: Also he will be rolled in salt. And sprayed with vinegar. And then his head will be removed with machete. Dena Paszek, can you please tell this to Margo Kellen?

DENA: Sure.

LESHIK: Perhaps you can repeat back to me?

DENA: I can try.

LESHIK: Take your time.

DENA: . . . So basically the deal is that if Denny doesn't meet Balboa with the money, Balboa is going to stab Denny multiple times.

LESHIK: With screwdriver.

DENA: With a screwdriver, right.

LESHIK: Perhaps also he will use high-powered drill or fourteen-centimeter spike from railroad, which will be exploded into his liver and anus, but this is beside the point.

DENA: So after Balboa stabs Denny many times with said screwdriver, high-powered drill, and/or fourteen-centimeter railroad spike, he and his rottweiler—

LESHIK: Larry Johnson.

DENA: He and his rottweiler Larry Johnson will essentially rape him in the various holes.

LESHIK: Don't forget about Dudu and Sasha.

DENA: Who are they, again?

LESHIK: Rottweiler-style dog and cornsnake belonging to me. I am Leshik.

DENA: Right. So in addition to Balboa's rottweiler Larry Johnson, your rottweiler Dudu, and your cornsnake Sasha, will also participate in raping these multiple wounds.

LESHIK: And don't forget ferret.

DENA: Belonging to . . .

LESHIK: Booker T With Remedy.

DENA: Who is . . .

LESHIK: Fat black gangster from Brownsville, Brooklyn.

DENA: Right. So in addition to Balboa's rottweiler Larry Johnson, your rottweiler Dudu, and your cornsnake Sasha, a ferret belonging to a large African-American man from Brownsville, Brooklyn, known as Booker T With Remedy will also rape the various holes in Denny's body.

LESHIK: Correct.

DENA: Does the ferret have a name?

LESHIK: No but he have syphilis.

DENA: The fucking ferret has syphilis?

LESHIK: He have syphilis, gonorrhea and bad breath. Keep going please.

DENA: Led by Balboa, after a motley complement of various canines, reptiles and a nameless, venereal, halitosis-addled rodent belonging to Booker T With Remedy essentially gang-bangs the holes in Denny's body, he will be rolled in salt and sprayed with vinegar.

LESHIK: And then?

DENA: And then his head will be chopped off.

LESHIK: With machete.

DENA: With a machete.

LESHIK: You understand.

DENA: I think I do. Wow. But can I ask a question?

LESHIK: Of course.

DENA: Will you be taking part in the production or sexual brutalization of the various screwdriver, high-powered drill, and railroad spike holes?

LESHIK: No. Only Balboa and Larry Johnson and Dudu and Sasha—

DENA: And the syphilitic, halitosis-addled ferret belonging to Booker T With Remedy.

LESHIK: Correct.

DENA: The large African-American gangsta from Brownsville.

LESHIK: Very good.

DENA: But Dudu is your rottweiler and Sasha is your cornsnake.

LESHIK: Yes.

DENA: So you are in some way a willing participant in these morally abominable activities.

LESHIK: I do not own snowmobile.

DENA: Of course you don't. One more thing.

LESHIK: Yes.

DENA: Is Balboa animal or human?

LESHIK: Balboa is human.

DENA: And who is he exactly?

LESHIK: He is boss. And he have very large penis.

DENA: Oh. Good for him.

LESHIK: Like great Polish horse.

DENA: And Balboa will be the one stabbing Denny several times with a screwdriver.

LESHIK: This is true, Dena Paszek.

DENA: In order to produce a number of holes into which he will insert his enormous horse penis.

LESHIK: Polish horse penis.

DENA: Of course.

LESHIK: Because there is also the Russian horse and the Turkish horse. The Polish horse is the most superior.

DENA: I'll have to remember that. Can I ask a practical question?

LESHIK: Yes.

DENA: Why the need for all the holes? I mean, why not just rape Denny in the ass and be done with it?

LESHIK: Because so many holes will produce more robust categories of pain.

DENA: I see.

LESHIK: Do not be mistaken, Dena Paszek. Also they will make love to his anus and his mouth many, many times. So many

times you can't even count. And sometimes Balboa will
make love to a person in the cheeks or in the eye or brain.

DENA: Interesting. How much money does Denny owe Balboa?

LESHIK: I do not know this.

DENA: Do you know how this debt was amassed?

LESHIK: I cannot say.

DENA: It's probably a lot of money to justify such a specific and
thorough punishment.

LESHIK: It is probably very much money.

DENA: Can I ask if it's drug-related?

LESHIK: I am sorry, Dena Paszek, but I am only the messenger.

DENA: Leshik The Messenger.

LESHIK: Yes.

DENA: And what will you be doing while all of this stabbing and
fucking is going on, Leshik The Messenger?

LESHIK: I most likely play 2003 John Madden NFL Game Boy.
Or study *Hot Rod* magazine.

DENA: I see.

LESHIK: But after the lovemaking maybe I take picture of Denny
Kellen's head on broomstick with new Ford Ikon Finesse
digital camera.

DENA: And you have no problem telling me all of this, knowing
that you are sharing possibly incriminating information.

LESHIK: I have no problem, no.

DENA: Why not?

LESHIK: Because I don't.

DENA: But what if I were to call the police?

LESHIK: I do not think you will do this.

DENA: Why not?

LESHIK: Because you seem like nice person.

DENA: Oh. Well, thank you.

LESHIK: You're welcome . . . Perhaps later you and Leshik can
eat rice pudding at Boleslaw's.

DENA: Who is Boleslaw?

LESHIK: He is my blood brother. He owns twenty-four-hours Polish diner on Second Avenue.

DENA: I'm afraid I have other plans.

LESHIK: Perhaps another time then.

DENA: Perhaps.

LESHIK: Because you are very handsome person, Dena Paszek. You have skin like vanilla ice mountain.

DENA: Oh. Thanks. I think.

LESHIK: Some day we go to Coney Island and ride the hot dog and eat foot-long Ferris Wheel.

(He hands her the crystal swan, turns to exit.)

DENA: Leshik.

LESHIK: Yes.

DENA: Can I ask how you got into the building?

LESHIK: I possess keys.

DENA: Whose keys?

LESHIK: Keys belonging to Denny Kellen.

DENA: Why do you have his keys?

LESHIK: Because I am good at my job.

DENA: I thought you were just a messenger.

LESHIK: Messenger-slash-key-collector. Now I go hunt. Goodbye.

DENA: Bye.

(Leshik exits toward the stairwell. Kevin opens his door.)

LESHIK: Hello.

(Leshik exits down the stairs.)

KEVIN: Hey, Dena.

DENA: Hi.

KEVIN: . . . Kevin.

DENA: Kevin, right.

KEVIN: How've you been?

DENA: Good, I've been good. And you?

KEVIN: Pretty good. Tryin' to stay cool. August, you know? If it's not the humidity it's the mosquitoes . . . So did Margo give you the book?

DENA: She did, yeah.

KEVIN: *Prisoner of Azkaban.* Signed first edition.

DENA: I saw that. Thanks.

KEVIN: I remember you sayin' how you were into J. K. Rowling and books and stuff?

DENA: Books are basically my whole life.

KEVIN: Well, there you go.

(Margo appears in her doorway. Her hair is wet. She is freshly showered. She is holding her purse and Dena's purse.)

MARGO *(Referring to the crystal swan)*: What are you doing with that?

DENA: I was thinking about taking it out for a walk. Margo, I really think you need to change your locks.

MARGO: Was Denny just here?

DENA: No. We can talk about it later.

KEVIN: You need me to call a locksmith?

DENA: Yes.

MARGO: No. Why do you have my swan?

DENA: I thought I saw a crack in it and I brought it out here. The harsh light is better for identifying imperfections.

MARGO *(Taking the swan)*: Is there a crack in it?

DENA: I don't think so.

MARGO *(Examining the swan)*: Did you drop it or something?

DENA: No. I was just looking at it when you were in the shower.

(Margo takes the swan into the apartment. An awkward pause between Kevin and Dena. Then:)

KEVIN: Wizards.

DENA *(Echoing)*: Wizards.

KEVIN *(Loud, to Margo)*: So what's the verdict—locksmith or no locksmith?

DENA (*Loud, to Margo*): Margo, I really think you should call a locksmith.

MARGO (*To Dena, from inside the apartment*): We only have fifteen minutes to get to the movie.

(*Margo reenters the hallway, shuts her door, locks it.*)

KEVIN (*To Dena*): Maybe we can grab coffee sometime. Like Starbucks or whatever. Talk some *Potter*.

DENA: Sure.

KEVIN: Excellent.

MARGO: Bye, Kevin.

(*Margo and Dena exit down the stairwell. Ido, Rahel's husband, a dark Israeli man, well-dressed, impressively built, enters the hall from upstairs.*)

KEVIN: Mr. Levy.

IDO: Hello.

KEVIN: Everything okay upstairs?

IDO: Everything is fine.

KEVIN: No more mice?

IDO: We catch one two days ago, but we find feces around sink this morning.

KEVIN: Like I told you before, the building is a hundred and fifty years old. We're gonna have our share of mice.

IDO: I understand. My wife is terrified, that is all.

KEVIN: I got a new exterminator coming after Labor Day, and the guy's supposed to be really good, so . . .

IDO: Thank you, Kevin. I know you are trying, and my wife and I appreciate it.

KEVIN: Anything else?

IDO: No.

KEVIN: Enjoy the rest of your day.

IDO: Also enjoy yours.

(Kevin enters his apartment, closes the door.

  Ido stands there, gathers himself, takes a deep breath, and crosses to Marty's door, knocks. Lucas answers. There is a small transistor radio in his lap playing Beyoncé's "Crazy in Love.")

LUCAS: Can I help you?

IDO: You are Lucas?

LUCAS: Lucas I am.

IDO: I am Ido, Rahel's husband. We live in Apartment Six. How are you?

LUCAS: Fine. And you?

IDO: Not so fine.

LUCAS: Sorry to hear that.

IDO: Thank you for your sympathy.

LUCAS: What can I do you for?

IDO: Can you turn that off, please?

(Lucas turns off the radio.)

Thank you . . . My wife tell me that you invite her over. To watch pornographic movies and play thumb wrestle. Is this true?

LUCAS: Not really.

IDO: What is not true about this?

LUCAS: The porn part. I mean I have tons of the stuff, but I was thinking we could start out with *Bedknobs and Broomsticks*, *Chitty Chitty Bang Bang*—that kind of thing.

IDO: *Chitty Chitty Bang Bang* is porn!

LUCAS: Some might call it porn, but, no, it's actually a classic Disney family film from the late sixties. You're obviously confusing it with *Pirate Smitty's Gang Bang*, the underground X-rated buccaneer masterpiece from the middle-late-nineties. It was considered quite the T-and-A swashbuckler.

IDO: Why would you do this?

LUCAS: Why would I invite your wife over to watch a movie?

IDO: Yes, please explain.

LUCAS: I don't know, Ido. We're neighbors?

IDO: You hurt her feelings.

LUCAS: Did I?

IDO: Yes, very much. I am in New Brunswick, New Jersey, and she calls me crying like child. This is not right. Rahel is beautiful person. She is polite and cares for others. This does not make sense to me.

LUCAS: She obviously misunderstood something.

IDO: Do you have no respect for her?

LUCAS: Because I invited her over to thumb wrestle? What's wrong with that?

IDO: What is wrong with inviting my wife into your apartment to put your thumbs in her vagina and anus?

LUCAS: You obviously have no idea what thumb wrestling is.

IDO: It is disgusting, this thumb wrestling, and you humiliate Rahel. I request that you apologize to my wife.

LUCAS: You do?

IDO: Yes.

LUCAS: Seriously?

IDO: Seriously.

LUCAS: . . . Okay.

IDO: Thank you.

LUCAS: Would you prefer this to be done in writing?

IDO: In person, please.

LUCAS: Like right now?

IDO: Yes.

LUCAS: Are you sure?

IDO: I am sure, yes.

LUCAS: Okay.

IDO (*Loud*): Rahel?

(*Rahel emerges from the stairwell. She slowly approaches Lucas and Ido, her hands behind her back, head down.*)

Our neighbor Lucas would like to apologize to you.

(Lucas stares at her a moment.)

LUCAS: Rahel?

RAHEL: Yes, Lucas?

LUCAS: I am so . . .

(Lucas unzips his pants.)

. . . unbelievably . . .

(Lucas pulls his balls through the opening, just his balls.)

. . . sorry.

IDO: What are you doing?

LUCAS: I'm apologizing. Can't you feel the regret?

IDO: Put your balls back!

(Lucas turns the radio back on and dances with his balls. The song is Kelly Osbourne's cover of "Papa Don't Preach.")

Put them back, please!

(Lucas keeps his balls out. Rahel covers her eyes. Ido seizes the radio, turns it off.)

I bring my wife to live with me here because I am told the people are good people. Nice people. I have to work every day. Sometimes for many hours. Sometimes I have to go on train to Connecticut or New Jersey. Sometimes to Boston, Massachusetts. Rahel doesn't yet have many friends. She does not speak the language so well. She study hard to learn English so she can have conversation. So she can be good neighbor and get job as teacher. She is good wife. She is a beautiful person. I want Rahel to have nice time. To be respected by others.

(Lucas says nothing.)

Please put your balls back.

LUCAS: Has anyone ever spit in your face?

IDO *(Shocked, hurt)*: Why would you say this to me?

LUCAS: I asked you if anyone's ever spit in your face.

IDO: You have your balls out and now you wish to spit in my face?

(Lucas musters a loogie.)

Do it. If you must.

(They stare at each other. Suddenly, at exactly 4:14 P.M. EST, all electric and digital sounds from the building cease: TV, radios, the thrum of air conditioners. The overhead light in the hallway flickers and goes out, revealing only silhouetted figures in the hallway, though there is some light from the window.

In the dark we hear the sound of Lucas spitting in Ido's face.)

RAHEL: Ido . . . Ido . . . What is happening, Ido.

IDO: Go upstairs, Rahel.

RAHEL: Ido, please.

IDO: Rahel, go upstairs, please!

(Kevin's door opens. He is holding a flashlight. Its beam illuminates the hall, arcs across Lucas and then Ido's face, which is wet. Lucas hasn't moved, nor has Ido.)

KEVIN: Everyone all right out here?

IDO: We are fine.

RAHEL *(From the stairwell)*: Ido!

(Ido produces a handkerchief, wipes his face, exits up the stairwell. Kevin trains the flashlight beam on Lucas.)

LUCAS: What.

(Kevin says nothing, holds the flashlight beam on Lucas's face.)

8:00 P.M.
Total darkness in the hallway. Margo and Lucas.

LUCAS: Can you see me?
MARGO: No. Can you see me?
LUCAS: I can't see anything . . . Pass the wine?

(She does so. He drinks.)

Is this French or Italian?
MARGO: I think it's Australian.
LUCAS: Kangaroo piss.
MARGO: Could do worse for six bucks.
LUCAS: How you feelin'? The oxy kick in yet?
MARGO: I just took it a few minutes ago.
LUCAS: . . . So the movie was good?
MARGO: It had promise in the same way that a quarter-pounder
    has beef, but the power went out about twelve minutes into
    it.

(A flashlight is turned on, is trained on Margo's face. In the brief light we see that she is sitting with her back against the wall, facing Lucas. They are across the hall from each other, in profile.)

Turn that thing off.

(Lucas turns the flashlight off.)

LUCAS: Pretty cool, right? The dark? It's like the hallway knows our thoughts.

MARGO: Sometimes I think this is what it's like for the baby. The little thing just floating in blackness. No thoughts. No feelings. Just blissfully, blindly floating.

LUCAS: You think you'll be a good mother?

MARGO: God I hope so.

LUCAS: You will be.

MARGO: How do you know?

LUCAS: I can just tell.

MARGO: Lately I barely take care of myself.

LUCAS: I'm a pretty good judge of character.

MARGO: You are, huh?

LUCAS: Yeah, I may be an asshole but I know people. I'm like a judge-of-character ninja.

MARGO: I'm so selfish.

LUCAS: Since when?

MARGO: I sit on my ass all day.

LUCAS: A lot of people sit on their ass.

MARGO: Asses.

LUCAS: A lot of people sit on their asses. It's one of our national pastimes.

MARGO: I could be doing more is all I'm saying.

LUCAS: Margo, you're six-and-a-half-months pregnant. You're supposed to sit on your ass all day. And like knit and make lanyards. It's not like you're not working. How many books are you copyediting right now?

MARGO: Four.

LUCAS: Four? That's crazy! You wanna talk about selfishness—

MARGO: We're not talking about Denny.

LUCAS: Okay. What should we talk about?

MARGO: I don't know. Anything.

LUCAS: We could talk about how bad I smell.

MARGO: Or how bad I smell.

LUCAS: Or how bad my farts smell.

MARGO: Oh, let's not.

LUCAS: We could talk about the ghost.

MARGO: Ooh, a ghost. Blackouts and ghosts.

LUCAS: And cheap Australian wine.

MARGO: And oxycotton. Tell me about the ghost.

LUCAS: Apparently she was some girl who hung herself back in the fifties. An actress who went insane.

MARGO: Was she famous?

LUCAS: All that's known about her is she was an actress and that she was from Darien, Connecticut.

MARGO: Have you ever seen her?

LUCAS: No, but Marty has.

MARGO: Like in the bathroom mirror?

LUCAS: Like in this hallway. Sometimes he sees her sitting at the piano. Sometimes he sees her face in the wall. Marty says she has long dark hair and what he describes as big UFO eyes. She wears a pale summer dress with little flowers on it. Sometimes he hears her crying in the middle of the night. But he's a lonely old queen with an active imagination.

MARGO: It's probably me he's hearing across the hall. Half kidding, keep going.

LUCAS: He claims that every so often he can hear her pacing in the hallway.

MARGO: And then what?

LUCAS: Nothing.

MARGO: That's it?

LUCAS: That's it.

MARGO: All she does is sit at the piano, occasionally embed herself in a wall, weep a little and pace the hallway? No erotic succubus visits? No blood oozing down the bedroom door? Pretty lame ghost.

LUCAS: Funny thing is that Marty's somehow convinced Mr. Yamagushi to keep his rent down because of it.

MARGO: Wow. Maybe I should try that one? I want a ghost! So much for tenant rights. Gimme a good old-fashioned motherfucking poltergeist!

(They drink.)

LUCAS: Do you really cry in the middle of the night?

MARGO: Sometimes I wake myself up.

LUCAS: How long has that been going on?

MARGO: Long enough.

LUCAS: But we don't talk about my brother.

MARGO: We're not talking about your brother.

(The frantic sound of a pigeon flying by over their heads, in the hallway. They are freaked-out. They laugh. The wine is accidentally knocked over.)

LUCAS: Was that a pigeon?

MARGO: I think it is.

LUCAS: A fucking pigeon. Jesus . . . So can I make a confession?

MARGO: Sure.

LUCAS: I think about you all the time.

MARGO: You do?

LUCAS: Yes.

MARGO: What do you think about?

(He says nothing.)

What, Lucas?

LUCAS: I don't know if this is such a good idea.

MARGO: Tell me. You think about what.

LUCAS: Um . . . making love to you.

MARGO: Oh.

LUCAS: Does that shock you?

(She doesn't answer.)

I'm sorry.

MARGO: It is a little shocking.

LUCAS: Margo, I've been in love with you from the first moment I saw you. You and Denny had just driven home from Kenyon. It was Christmas break your junior year. You guys came into the kitchen through the garage. You were wearing a blue ski parka and your hair was really short and your face was puffy. You had a little line down your cheek from sleeping on the seatbelt. I had just been in the living room helping my mom with the tree and I saw you and it was like everything else faded away.

MARGO: Bullshit.

LUCAS: I'm not lying, Margo. Everything faded. The walls. The kitchen table. The linoleum floor. It was like I had been visited by someone from a dream. Just you in your blue ski parka. Floating there.

MARGO: Were you high?

LUCAS: I was after you walked in. You spent five days in Cleveland and all I cared about was trying to find ways to justify being in the same room as you. To get close enough to smell your hair. Which actually happened once after dinner when you were clearing the table. I was rinsing plates for the dishwasher and you brushed past me and I finally smelled it.

MARGO: It probably stunk. I think I showered like ten times that semester.

LUCAS: It smelled like apples.

MARGO: Really?

LUCAS: You brushed past me and I smelled apples and I grew a third lung. I was a fucking zitty-faced junior in high school and I had fallen head-over-heels in love-at-first-sight with the woman who would wind up marrying my only brother. How doomed is that.

Your wedding was probably the worst day of my life. I don't even want to tell you what was going through my head as you were coming down the aisle. I was a groomsman and I thought my heart was going to turn into a peach pit and fall out of my tuxedo sleeve. I think I spent the next year trying to kill that vision of you in that dress. Every time I closed my eyes I would see you.

. . . Margo, every morning when I wake up all I can think about is you. How you're doing, if your back hurts, if your feet are swollen, what music you might be listening to, what you're wearing, what you're not wearing . . .

Why do you think I wanted to spend the summer here? It was perfect—I'd be across the hall! I mean it doesn't even make any sense—I'm stuck in a wheelchair on the third floor of a fucking walk-up. I spend more time looking out the window than an international spy. I've left the building once this entire summer. July Fourth weekend. I humped down the stairs on my hands and Marty wheeled me over to Sixth Avenue and I ate a slice at Ray's Pizza and then we went and watched a basketball game at the West 4th Street courts. And the whole time I wanted to be back here because you and Dena had gone to see Denny's band play and I knew you'd be coming home.

Sometimes I just sit on the other side of Marty's door and wait to hear the sound of someone coming up the stairs, hoping it's you. It's the main reason I've grown to hate everyone in this building: because they're never you when they come up the stairs. This floor is like a fucking prison, but I don't care because I get to be near you.

MARGO: . . . Can I ask a question?

LUCAS: Of course.

MARGO: Regarding the lovemaking thing: Can you still . . . ?

LUCAS: I can still control my bowels and my bladder and I can still get an erection. The bullet somehow spared all that. I thank God every day for the half centimeter.

MARGO: Since when have you believed in God?

LUCAS: Getting shot can reverse even the most tenacious spiritual cynic. You should've heard me in the medevac. I was making deals with our Holy Father like he was some high-powered lawyer. If you let me walk again I'll be a better person. If you let me fuck again I'll vote Democrat.

MARGO: So now you're a lefty asshole.

LUCAS: I think The Hunt produced enough lefty assholes to start a softball league.

MARGO: Welcome home meanies.

LUCAS: Here's your state-of-the-art wheelchair. Bill Bradley's your man.

MARGO: Bill Bradley was 2000. John Kerry's our man now.

LUCAS: Bill Bradley, John Kerry, Smokey the Bear. They're all the same to me. To be honest, I didn't even vote in 2000.

MARGO: But you will now.

LUCAS: Fuckin'-A right I will. God spared my dick.

MARGO: Did you really think you were going to find that guy?

LUCAS: Who, Bin Laden? I guess at first I thought we might. In like some video game sort of way: "There he is hiding behind that almond tree. A thousand points if you shoot his turban off."

MARGO: Isn't he supposed to be really tall?

LUCAS: He's like six-eight or something.

MARGO: Dena thinks he's sexy.

LUCAS: He's probably hung like a walrus.

(They drink.)

The thing about getting shot is that you feel it before you hear it. The bullet travels faster than the speed of sound. And in most combat situations you have no idea who shot you, so you can never put a face to it . . .

MARGO: How did it happen?

LUCAS: We got ambushed. And I was one of the dipshits who got shot.

MARGO: You think we'll ever find him?

LUCAS: Bin Laden? Who knows? Who cares? At this point, aside from satisfying some Old-Testament vindication, what would it accomplish? For all we know he's probably working at a Sunglasses Hut in a stripmall in Palm Springs.

MARGO: I'm so sorry that happened to you, Lucas.

LUCAS: In a few weeks I'll be down in Sarasota, living about a half mile from your in-laws, drinking G-and-Ts and staring out at the luxurious foliage of Merrill Gardens assisted-living community with a bunch of other rich cripples.

MARGO: Why did you enlist, anyway? I mean, you have your degree.

LUCAS: Yeah, a lotta good that does.

MARGO: You're one of the smartest people I know.

LUCAS: So I've read a few books and I've written a few papers. Joyce was a genius, Shakespeare a poet, Hemingway liked to hunt, where does that get you.

MARGO: You could teach.

LUCAS: And turn into one of those lonely, middle-aged professors who ends up arranging his life for the sole purpose of sleeping with naive freshman girls from Madison, Wisconsin? I can just see it: the recycled syllabus; my office overgrown with ungraded papers; my hair turning a yellowish gray; jowls; hemorrhoids; a coronary while wheeling myself to a faculty meeting.

MARGO: One of your freshman hotties could wheel you. Then at least you'd avoid the coronary.

LUCAS: Nofuckingthankyou.

(Shouting comes from the hallway.)

MARGO: I wonder what's going on out there.

LUCAS: Sounds like Mardi Gras.

MARGO: People need the smallest excuse to go bananas.

(Beat.)

Whatever happened to that physical therapist who was coming around earlier in the summer?

LUCAS: Who, Maureen?

MARGO: Talk about a hottie.

LUCAS: She smelled.

MARGO: She did?

LUCAS: Yeah. She had hairy armpits. I don't like that hippie shit.

MARGO: She had a cute little body though. Pretty face. Big blue eyes. I thought she liked you.

LUCAS: She stank.

MARGO: You're terrible . . . What do you like?

LUCAS: I like you.

MARGO: You wouldn't if you spent any real time with me.

LUCAS: Guys in my unit had pictures of their wives, their girl-friends. I had a fucking picture of you and my brother standing in front of a waterfall . . . I don't know what I'm gonna do when I have to go.

(After a pause, from Margo we hear what could be construed as weeping. And silence. And the sound of movement.

The ghost of Rose Hathaway Bumper emerges from the stairwell. She sits on the windowsill and then starts up the stairs. She wears white kid gloves.

In silhouette, we see that Margo is standing over Lucas. She is touching his face. He is staring up at her. He places his hand on hers. She bends down, kisses him fully on the mouth. She places Lucas's hand on her heart and her hand over his. The Ghost of Rose Hathaway Bumper quietly exits up the stairs. We then hear Lucas whisper, "I love you," over and over.

The sound of footsteps coming up the stairs. Kevin enters with a flashlight, the light cutting through the darkness.)

KEVIN: Everyone okay up here?
MARGO: We're fine.

(From the flashlight we see that Margo and Lucas are now separated.)

KEVIN: Marty okay?
LUCAS: I don't know. He went out.
KEVIN: You got a landline, right?
LUCAS: Yeah, why?
KEVIN: Because once your cell phone dies there's no recharging.

(Kevin sets a bunch of candles down, the kind in mason jars, and a few books of matches.)

Help yourself to these. Apparently the whole eastern seaboard is wiped out. I would advise eating whatever's in your fridge before it spoils.

(Darkness.)

Later, before midnight.

A thin table with a makeshift tablecloth has been brought out into the hallway. Candles are lit: a few on the table; a few on the piano; one in the stairwell. There is very little light coming in from the window, moonlight at best. The table boasts everything from the fridges of the three apartments: jars of pickles, juices, quarts of milk, jars of olives, cold cuts, plates of cheeses, a salmon, ice cream, grapes, a few bottles of wine and the case of beer Lucas stole from Kevin's apartment. Seated around the table in mismatched chairs are Lucas, Margo, Kevin and Dena. Margo is especially loaded now, with the alcohol really combining effectively with the oxycotton pill. Using a flashlight as a mike, or maybe a bottle of salad dressing, she sings "The Night the Lights Went Out in Georgia." Dena leads the choruses and Kevin and Lucas join her, learning the song as they go. This is good fun with lots of dancing and shenanigans.

Ido enters and they stop singing.

KEVIN: Ido. What's up?

IDO: Have you seen Rahel?

MARGO: I'm afraid we haven't.

IDO: Are you sure?

KEVIN: Pretty sure, yeah.

LUCAS *(Looking under the table)*: Rahel, you under there?

(Ido does not find this funny.)

KEVIN: Somethin' wrong?

IDO: I fall asleep and when I wake up she is gone.

DENA: Maybe she went out to get candles?

MARGO: Yeah, maybe she wennout to get some candy.

KEVIN: They're handing out candles over at St. Augustine's on Houston Street.

IDO: We have candles.

MARGO: I want some candy. I wanna jollyrancher. Yum.

DENA: Maybe she needed some air and didn't want to disturb you.

IDO: She would leave a note.

LUCAS *(Looking under the table again)*: Rahel, come out of there now!

DENA: Lucas . . .

IDO: It's been almost two hours. She never leaves like that.

KEVIN: I wouldn't panic, Ido.

MARGO: No panic, Ido. No panic.

IDO: I must go look for her. If she comes back, please ask her to wait here.

(Ido exits. There is a tense silence and then Lucas grabs the flashlight, starts singing again. Lucas wheels over to the piano and starts to feel out the chords. Margo and Dena are dancing now, drunk. Kevin stands and sort of moves his arms around.

Marty enters from the stairwell with a young African-American man dressed in basketball gear, a baseball hat cocked sideways. The music ceases. The young African-American man is carrying a plastic bag from Foot Locker, containing a box of new shoes Marty had bought him.)

LUCAS: Marty.

MARGO: Thank God, Marty. We were worried sick.

(She hugs him dramatically, laughs, sits, almost falling off her chair.)

Ooops! I almost fell down!

(She laughs, then does fall on her butt, on the floor. A scary moment.)

DENA: Careful, Margo.

(Margo bursts out laughing hysterically, eventually stops. Kevin helps her off the floor.)

MARTY: Everyone, this is Cory. Cory, this is Lucas, that's Margo, her friend Dena, and that's Kevin.

CORY: 'Sup.

LUCAS: 'Sup, yo.

DENA: Lucas behave.

KEVIN: We're all glad you're okay, Mr. Kubiak.

MARTY: We're just fine, right Cory?

CORY: We straight.

LUCAS: Where'd you go?

MARTY: Oh, here and there, right Cory?

CORY: Here, there and everywhere.

LUCAS: I see you did a little shopping. *(To Cory)* Got yourself a little schwag bag?

(Awkward pause.)

MARGO *(Giggling)*: Does anybody have any candy?

DENA: Margo's had a little too much to drink.

MARGO: I have not! I wanna jollyrancher!

MARTY: Looks like you all are having yourselves a good time.

LUCAS: I brought your lunch meat out here. Figured we'd eat it before it spoiled.

KEVIN: We all raided our fridges. Party on the third floor.

DENA: Don't tell the super!

MARGO: Superduperpooperscooper!!!

(They all laugh. It dies. Then:)

KEVIN: Pull up a chair, Mr. Kubiak.

MARGO: Yeah, pull up a chair, Mary. I mean Marty. Pull it up.

MARTY: We're pretty tired, but thanks for the offer.

(Marty leads Cory to his apartment.)

And don't feel like you have to keep it down out here, because we don't mind the noise, do we Cory?

CORY: It's gonna get heated where we goin' so you might as well get heated out here.

(Marty keys into the apartment, opens the door.)

Nice to meet y'all.

EVERYONE: Nice to meet you.

(Marty and Cory enter Marty's apartment, close the door.
    Everyone bursts out laughing. Lucas wheels over to the door, listens. Marty opens the door.)

MARTY: Yes?

LUCAS: Nothing. I was just . . . nothing.

(Marty closes the door in his face.
    Kevin turns on a battery-operated transistor radio. They tune into a report of what's going on with the blackout—the enormity of it. Outside, sirens can be heard, mayhem. Kevin crosses to the window, peers down at the courtyard.)

KEVIN: Some guy's in the courtyard walking around in scuba gear.

(He opens the window.)

(Shouting down) What the fuck are you doin', bro?
MAN IN COURTYARD *(Off)*: Looking for the leitmotif!

(Kevin closes the window.)

KEVIN: Fucking lunatic.

(From Marty's apartment, sounds of two men having sex. Lucas turns the radio off. They all listen. It should be somehow conveyed that this is Marty's first sexual experience in many years. Marty can be heard climaxing. The sex ends.)

DENA: Hey, let's play a game.
LUCAS: Let's not.
DENA: No, let's. Let's play the if-there-was-one-way-you-could-change-your-life-what-would-it-be game.
KEVIN: Is that a game?
DENA: It is tonight. One choice you could make. One destiny-changing action.
LUCAS: I would shit my pants and set myself on fire.

(Margo makes the noise of someone shitting his pants and then lighting himself on fire.)

DENA: No, seriously. I'm being serious.
KEVIN: One choice.
DENA: One choice. And not something you would change about the past. Something you would do right now. Today. Tonight. I'll go first.

(She thinks for a moment.)

(To Kevin) I would invite myself over and fuck your brains out.

KEVIN: That's my answer, too.

DENA: But not because I'd necessarily want to.

MARGO: Then why?

LUCAS: Because she would want to see his flashlight collection.

DENA: Because it would immediately change my life.

LUCAS: People fuck each other's brains out every day.

MARGO: But she hasn't been laid in a year.

DENA: Thanks, Margo.

MARGO: I'm just saying. Sex isn't a casual thing for you.

KEVIN: Hey, good things can come out of chaos.

DENA: And so can bad things, but that's my point. We get so . . . stuck in our lives. I've been working at the same publishing company for eight years. I walk the same route to work. I take the elevator to the same floor, talk to the same agents on the phone, attend the same boring editorial meetings. I eat my lunch at roughly the same time every day. On Saturdays I go to Film Forum or to a play at Lincoln Center and I have Sunday brunch with a sociable articulate friend whose outfit often equals his or her capacity to charm, and then I usually come over here and spend a few hours with Margo complaining about all of it and nothing really changes.

LUCAS: Sounds like you really need to get laid.

DENA: I mean everyone here's probably been through some cursory existential philosophy class. We've studied our bit of Sartre and Kierkegaard and we've read William Barrett and talked about action and inaction and what it means to be alive and how most of us wind up middle-aged zombies, etcetera, etcetera, but if you really stop to think about it—if you really consider the possibility, isn't it amazing how, on a candlelit night without the comfort of cable television or the internet or your porn collection, or your favorite halogen lamp, whathaveyou, isn't it amazing how one irrational choice could change your life?

Let's say I did go into Kevin's apartment and fuck his brains out.

KEVIN: Okay.

DENA: Any number of things could happen. I could start shrieking for joy. I could get vertigo. I could freak out and curl into a ball.

MARGO: You could have an orgasm.

DENA: I could have an Olympic orgasm. I could spontaneously get my period.

KEVIN: That would suck.

LUCAS: You could get a yeast infection and wind up spooning yogurt into your vagina.

DENA: I could! I could get a fucking yeast infection and wind up spooning yogurt into my vagina!

MARGO: You could have an orgasm.

DENA: I could have multiple outerbody, extraterrestrial orgasms till my ears bled and realize I've met my soul mate. *(To Kevin)* We could fall in love.

KEVIN: Okay.

DENA: The possibilities are endless.

MARGO: But would you really change?

LUCAS: Or would you just get a yeast infection? Or herpes?

DENA: Who knows? What's important is taking the leap.

MARGO: But there would be repercussions. Even if you two fell in love there would be repercussions.

DENA: But I'm saying bring it on. Bring the motherfucking repermotherfuckingcussions on.

LUCAS *(Finishing Dena's sentence)*: Yo.

MARGO: Kevin, what about you?

KEVIN: I would fuck Dena . . . I mean make love to Dena . . . Tonight . . . In my bed. To the Ramones . . . "End of the Century" on continuous replay . . . No, "Rocket to Russia" and then "End of the Century." . . . And she would have a thunderous orgasm . . . Like the kind you read about in magazines . . . Our bodies would turn blue in the moonlight

. . . And it would be legendary . . . By the way is this my beer? This is my fucking beer.

LUCAS *(To Margo)*: What about you?

MARGO: I don't know. The idea of taking action right now is pretty paralyzing.

KEVIN: Oh, come on, after all that? You gotta play, Margo.

DENA: It's just a game.

LUCAS: She would change the locks.

MARGO: That's too easy.

DENA: You could shave your head.

MARGO: No.

DENA: Or your pussy. You could shave your pussy.

KEVIN: Eat a cockroach.

DENA: Apply to grad school. Fly to Africa. Join the Peace Corps.

MARGO: I would get rid of it.

DENA: . . . Margo

MARGO: No, Dena, you wanted to play this game, so let's really play it. I would go into some rat-infested alley, squat over a garbage can and shit the thing out of my body. But that's not actually going to happen, so while you two can go fuck each other's brains out I'm left with very few options.

DENA: I'm sorry, Margo. That was insensitive.

KEVIN: What about you, Lucas?

LUCAS: Margo knows what I would do.

KEVIN: Which is what?

(Lucas says nothing, simply stares at Margo.)

Come on, bro.

LUCAS: It's between me and Margo.

MARGO: Pass the wine, please.

(Kevin passes the wine. Margo takes a long drink. Cory enters from Marty's apartment, holding his Foot Locker bag.)

DENA: Hey, Cory.

CORY: Hey.

LUCAS: Where's Marty?

CORY: He fell out.

LUCAS: Meaning what exactly?

CORY: Meanin' he asleep.

LUCAS: Is he okay?

CORY: He fine, why?

KEVIN: He has health issues.

CORY: Health issues. What type of health issues?

LUCAS: He's a diabetic.

DENA: Don't worry, it's not contagious.

CORY: I know diabetes ain't contagious. You think I'm stupid? He fell out and now he asleep.

(Lucas wheels away from the table, toward Marty's apartment.)

Oh, you don't believe me?

(Lucas enters Marty's apartment.)

Damn. Put a nigga in the dark and suddenly he a criminal. I'd hate to see what y'all would do if I started blowin' these candles out . . . He did his business and then he fell asleep.

KEVIN: He did his business? What does that mean?

CORY: Whatchu think it means? He got his nut off and passed the fuck out.

(Lucas reenters the hallway.)

LUCAS: He's sound asleep.

CORY: With a big smile on his face, right?

(Lucas doesn't answer.)

So am I free to go?

DENA: You're more than welcome to join us.

CORY: Thanks, but I gotta work tomorrow.

KEVIN: No one's goin' to work tomorrow, Cory. Power's out on the whole eastern seaboard.

DENA: Where do you work?

CORY: At a job. Where you work?

DENA: Um, Viking.

CORY: You a Viking?

DENA: No, Viking Press. It's a publishing company.

CORY: Like books and shit?

DENA: Exactly.

CORY: Cool.

DENA: You sure you don't want to join us?

CORY: Naw, I gotta roll. But can I get a sandwich?

MARGO: Of course.

CORY: Thanks.

(He starts to make himself a sandwich.)

Some crazy stuff goin' on out there.

KEVIN: Like what?

CORY: People actin' foolish. Second Avenue like one big block party. Everyone sittin' in fronta restaraunts, half they clothes off, drinkin' forties, blastin' music, settin' off fireworks, gettin' blunted. Never seen so many candles in my life: birfday candles; church candles; big-ass torches and shit. Everyone actin' like it's the end of the world 'cause the lights went out.

(Cory finishes with the sandwich, wraps it in a napkin.)

DENA: Cory, if you could do one thing to change your life right now what would it be?

CORY: What?

DENA: One action you could take to make your life better?

CORY: You serious?

DENA: Yes, I'm serious.

LUCAS *(Mocking the rap lyric)*: She serious as a heart attack.

CORY: Yo, you a fuckin' asshole, ain't you.

LUCAS: You asking or telling me?

CORY: I'm telling you. You think being in that wheelchair gives you the right to be nasty to people?

LUCAS: Um, no.

CORY: Because that's how you act. Cripple or no cripple, I don't give a fuck about you. And I ain't no punk.

LUCAS: I didn't say you were.

CORY: But that's how you actin'. So fuck you.

DENA: Seriously, Cory, what would you do?

CORY: Fuck if I know. Make another sandwich. Can I get two?

KEVIN: Help yourself.

(He makes the second one in silence.

Lucas takes Margo's hand under the table. She doesn't resist. A cell phone rings. Margo takes her hand back, answers the phone.)

MARGO *(Into phone)*: Denny? . . . Hello? Yes, this is she . . . Uh-huh . . . Uh-huh . . . Uh-huh . . . Uh-huh . . . Uh-huh . . . Uh-huh . . . Uh-huh.

(She hangs up. Cory exits.)

(To Dena) Were you supposed to tell me something?

DENA: Tell you what?

MARGO: This guy said he spoke to you and that you were going to give me a message. About Denny.

DENA: Well he's lying.

MARGO: Are you sure?

DENA: The only thing he said was that you should change your locks and I already told you that.

(Marty enters, wearing a robe. He is disoriented, his hair is a mess.)

MARTY: Where'd he go?

(Silence.)

Where's Cory?

(Silence.)

Did he leave?

KEVIN: You just missed him, Mr. Kubiak.

MARTY: When?

DENA: A few minutes ago.

KEVIN: He made a coupla sandwiches and left.

MARTY: But he said he would stay. *(To Lucas)* Did you say something to him?

LUCAS: No.

MARTY: Are you lying? *(To the others)* Is he lying?

LUCAS: What would I say to him?

KEVIN: Mr. Kubiak, Lucas didn't say anything. I was right here.

MARTY: Well, did he say where he was going?

DENA: He said he had to work tomorrow.

MARTY: We were supposed to go to breakfast. And then we were gonna go up to Central Park and maybe to a museum . . . We were supposed to have breakfast. *(To Lucas)* What did you say to him?!

LUCAS: I didn't say anything, Marty.

MARTY: Yes you did yes you did yes you did . . .

(Marty starts to cry. He has to use the wall for support.)

KEVIN: Mr. Kubiak, come on now . . .

(Ido enters from the stairwell. He is moving slow, in shock, dejected:)

IDO: Rahel did not return?

KEVIN: We haven't seen her, Mr. Levy.

IDO: I am very worried. I walk all the way to the East River. All the way to Tompkins Square Park. *(To Lucas)* You did this. This is your fault . . .

(Denny runs into the hallway, screaming for his life, totally naked, bleeding from gashes carved into in his back, legs and shoulders. Leshik is chasing him, wielding a machete. Leshik is wild-eyed, equally crazed, speaking Polish. There is chaos around the table. Things fly, bottles are overturned. Denny throws things at Leshik—lunch meat, ice cream, the jar of pickles. He hits him, misses him. Denny bursts into his apartment, closes the door, locks it.

Leshik quickly produces Denny's keys, unlocks the door, goes in after him. We hear sounds of struggle, of Denny pleading for his life.

Lucas wheels in after them. More struggling, screaming.

Then, a gunshot.

And silence.

Kevin enters the apartment, quickly reenters the hallway.)

KEVIN: Somebody call an ambulance.

(Everyone is frozen.)

Somebody call a fucking ambulance!

(Marty quickly enters his apartment.

Denny enters the hallway on his hands and knees. He is still naked and his arm has been slashed but he's very much alive. He crawls to Margo, hugs her around the knees, his head down, a supplication.)

DENNY *(Sobbing)*: I'm sorry, I'm sorry, I'm sorry, I'm sorry, I'm sorry . . .

(Lucas wheels out, the gun in his lap. Margo pries Denny's hands from around her legs, steps away from him, crosses to the other side of the hallway. Lucas looks at Denny heaped on the floor, curled into a ball now, sobbing, still saying, "I'm sorry, I'm sorry, I'm sorry," over and over. Everyone else looks on, frozen in the candlelight. Marty reenters the hallway.)

MARTY: They're on their way.

(From the street, the sound of drums, crackling flames, mobs in the night.)

END

NURSING

Characters

TOUR GUIDE, Sandra

GUARD, U.S. Marshal Harris

LLOYD BOYD, the patient, thirty-two

NURSE ANDY, Andrew Woodcock

JOAN, a nurse, attractive, mid-thirties

JOE BOYD, Lloyd's brother

ERIN, the mother of Lloyd's son

JOURNALIST

Setting

A former tenement apartment building on the Lower East Side of Manhattan, 2053, now called The Mary Ellen Baird Museum of Disease and Nursing.

PART ONE

The winter.

At the box office, where the audience is gathering, a female Tour Guide gains everyone's attention. A Guard wands ticket holders as a security precaution. A red curtain is drawn across the performance area.

TOUR GUIDE: Welcome, everyone. I'm Sandra and I'm your tour guide for today's Grand Opening of The Mary Ellen Baird Museum of Disease and Nursing, and we're just so happy that you've decided to join us . . . Do I have everyone's attention? *(She waits for everyone to quiet)* . . . Thank you. While we're taking our seats I'd like to give you a brief history of the museum.

Mary Ellen Baird was a pediatrics, prison and hospice nurse from Elmira, New York, who spent thirty-five years in the nursing profession before her life was taken by a rare form of cancer at the young age of fifty-five. She passed away in 2027, two years before the cure for cancer was discovered, a turn of ugly poetry when you consider the fact that she spent her entire life healing others, whether they were afflicted children or AIDS-riddled death-row inmates.

Her oldest son, Peter, a wealthy entrepreneur in the alternative fuels business, purchased the building ten years ago and converted what was once a simple tenement into our esteemed museum. Mr. Baird did this in honor of his mother and it was important to him and the Baird family to create a live disease and nursing exhibit so that we would be reminded of the importance of an antiquated profession and the brutality of disease.

(She motions to the red curtain drawn in front of what appears to be a kind of playing space, perhaps thirty feet wide. A distinct white line running in front of the curtain marks a thirty-six-inch gap between the line and the curtain. Within that space stands an armed U.S. Marshal with an automatic weapon, wearing bulletproof torso armor. He is the same armed Guard who was wanding ticket holders. He stands at port arms, scanning the audience.)

So, are we all seated? *(She waits until everyone is seated and settled)* . . . Good. Just a little bit of business before we pull back the curtain. Your ticket is a license that entitles you to stay for as long as you like.

All recording apparatuses, including cell phones, video cameras and any other micromedia paraphernalia are prohibited. If you are caught operating one of these devices, Special U.S. Marshal Harris will rush you like an invigorated but highly agitated, fleet-footed animal. And they don't want that to happen, do they, Mr. Harris?

GUARD: No, Sandra, they do not want that to happen.

TOUR GUIDE: So, while you take in the exhibit, we at the museum ask that you consider your own health, the luxury of living in our disease-free world, and the importance of all those people who dedicated their lives to healing the sick and dying.

(The Tour Guide pulls the red curtain aside to reveal a thirty-foot-wide hermetically sealed glass window. At this point, the audience can't hear the activity on the other side of the glass, which features a dingy hospital room. A folded hospital bed has been wheeled off to the side, next to a chair. Dead center in the exhibit room is a mattress on the floor, a mess of bedding, a pillow. There are monitors, an IV rack, etc., assembled around the mattress. It feels a bit like a messy island of sloth. The actual exhibit room has been converted from a Lower East Side tenement hallway. There is an exposed toilet, like a military head, and a functioning shower nozzle, with a pate of ceramic tiles, a center drain, a handrail on the wall under the nozzle. Also under the shower nozzle, an orthopedic walker. As per the toilet, there is no stall or divider. It is clear that the room has been personalized to the tastes of the observed subject, that it has a smell, a lived-in history.

Pushed against the wall, opposite the toilet and shower, is an old upright piano. A doorway leads to an offstage nurses' station, where people can exit and enter.

A pair of swirling red lights, like ambulance lights, flash on opposite ends of the stage.)

The Black Death was one of the deadliest pandemics in human history, peaking in Europe between 1348 and 1350. It is widely thought to have been an outbreak of bubonic plague caused by the bacterium *Yersinia pestis*. Probably carried by fleas residing on the black rats that were regular passengers on merchant ships, it spread like wildfire throughout the Mediterranean and Europe.

It is estimated that the Black Death killed thirty to sixty percent of Europe's population. Symptoms included fevers of 101 to 105 degrees Fahrenheit, headaches, painful aching joints, nausea and vomiting, and a general feeling of malaise. Of those who contracted the Black Death, four out of five died within eight days.

Seven days ago, our subject, Lloyd Boyd, was transdermally inoculated with a controlled dose of Black Death and our nursing staff here at the museum has been busy tending to his health needs, which, as you can see, are currently quite considerable.

The swirling red lights signify that our subject, whom I will introduce in just a moment, is at his most contagious. Any nurse who comes into direct contact with him must observe the highest level of biosafety protocol. Note the mask, gloves and other coverings. This is a highly communicable situation, ladies and gentlemen, but one that we on this side of this glass are entirely safe from.

You are not allowed to touch the glass. We ask that you respect the white line. Fear not, the glass is hermetically sealed and you are completely safe, but in case there is an emergency, which is highly unlikely, there are medical masks under each of your chairs. You may put them on now, you may take them home, you may leave them—it's up to you.

(Lloyd Boyd, thirty-two, is being held down in his bed by a large male nurse, Nurse Andy, who is masked, all exposed flesh covered, his hands protected with rubber gloves. Lloyd wears a hospital garment, open in the back, and nothing else. He looks terrible, with dark circles under his eyes, a nubbed head. His skin is jaundiced and marked with black spots here and there. He is at the height of agony and looks as if he could explode at any moment.)

Mr. Boyd has signed a medical waiver of informed consent and is fully aware of the risks to his survival. Once the antidote is administered, he will become entirely asymptomatic within a few days.

Regarding Special U.S. Marshal Harris, the museum employs him because there have been several recent threats by an unnamed underground anarchist group who

wish to reintroduce various diseases, viruses and patho-
gens to the airborne world. Anyone who attempts to cross
the white line will be shot and killed.

Sound.

*(The sound on the other side of the glass kicks in and is
now amplified into the audience. Andy ultimately stabilizes
Lloyd, calms him, straps him to his mattress, injects him with
a fast-acting sedative that knocks him out.*

*Once Lloyd is unconscious, Andy cleans his wounds:
the lesions, the black spots on his neck and chest. Then he
administers the antidote.)*

As you can see, our capable nurse, Andrew Woodcock, who
hails from Coral Gables, Florida, has just administered
the antidote, which will take effect as soon as it enters the
bloodstream . . .

*(Andy holds Lloyd firmly by the shoulders, calming him,
doing everything in his power to help him.)*

And now Mr. Boyd is on the proverbial road to recovery.

(Music.)

The following morning.

Andy enters with a bouquet of flowers arranged in a vase, sets them on the floor.

ANDY: How are you feeling?

(Lloyd groans.)

Where is the pain exactly?

LLOYD: My lungs, my eyes, my tongue . . . my spine, my calves, my throat . . . my armpits, the soles of my feet.

ANDY *(Referring to the IV cartridge)*: I'd be happy to up your dosage.

LLOYD: Yes, please.

(Andy adjusts the cartridge, the IV bag, writes something down on Lloyd's chart, then treats Lloyd's skin wounds, his welts, his various bandages, checks his vitals.)

ANDY: Well, your vitals are good. You're most definitely bouncing back. You think you're up for some solid food?

LLOYD: What's on the menu?

ANDY: Today there's turkey breast, mashed potatoes and mixed vegetables.

LLOYD: Dessert?

ANDY: Assorted berries.

LLOYD: You mean lukewarm fruit cup. *(Trying to remember his name)* Andy, right?

ANDY: Yes, Andy.

LLOYD *(Suddenly smelling something)*: Do you smell that, Andy?

ANDY: Smell what?

LLOYD: It smells like something's in the wall.

ANDY: I don't smell anything.

(Beat.)

LLOYD: Who are the flowers from?

ANDY *(Reading from the attached card)*: Sister Mary Katherine Grace of Dubuque, Iowa. Do you know her?

LLOYD: Former college professor.

ANDY: What subject?

LLOYD: Lit Crit. Crazy lefty nun. She thought Hunter S. Thompson was the end-all-be-all. She would quote from *The Rum Diary* like it was Chaucer . . . When I enlisted in the Army she wrote me impassioned emails begging me to reconsider.

ANDY: Were you part of the bombing?

LLOYD: I got deployed four days after the worst of it.

ANDY: I can't even imagine it.

LLOYD: You can easily imagine it. There was a slew of video games so lifelike in their renderings they captured the quality of the vapor in the air.

ANDY: I don't play those things.

LLOYD: I imagine most nurses wouldn't.

ANDY: I guess we are an old-fashioned bunch.

LLOYD: You say that and I imagine a knitting circle.

ANDY: I do knit! I'm a good knitter!

(Beat.)

Did Sister Mary Katherine stay in touch with you?

LLOYD: She sent me emails every day I was over there. While I was picking through the rubble, trying not to inhale ash and bone dust, she was imploring me to come back to Iowa and pursue a master's degree. She thought I had a serious future in literature.

ANDY: The things you must have seen over there . . .

LLOYD: All the heavy action was over. It was mostly a cleanup mission. I spent twelve hours a day hiding behind an assisted-breathing mask.

ANDY: But you still must have seen stuff . . . The Director told me that after you came home you taught high school English.

LLOYD: Not much teaching was going on. Not much learning either.

ANDY: How long did you teach?

LLOYD: I made it through a semester and a half.

ANDY: You mind me asking all these questions?

LLOYD: Not really. But it's not very professional of you, Andy.

(Beat.)

ANDY: How's the pain, better?

(Lloyd nods.)

You know you really might be more comfortable in a hospital bed.

LLOYD: I prefer the floor.

(Awkward pause.)

ANDY: Hey, would you like me to get you some books?

LLOYD: No thanks.

ANDY: Why not?

LLOYD: Reading takes too much effort anymore. Besides I'm content being all dumb and blank-brained.

ANDY: I'd be happy to read to you.

LLOYD: . . . *Green Eggs and Ham.*

ANDY: I'll see what I can do . . . Do you need anything else?

LLOYD: Up?

(Andy retrieves his orthopedic walker, helps him sit up, get out of bed. Andy helps to guide the IV stand while Lloyd makes his way to the piano. Lloyd sits, starts to play. Andy takes the vase of flowers, crosses to the piano, sets them on the hood of the piano. Lloyd stops playing, considers the flowers, considers Andy, then continues playing as Andy looks on.

Suddenly three eggs fly against the glass and break.

The Guard chases someone down into the stairwell.

Lloyd and Andy are oblivious to the action on the other side of the glass. Lloyd continues playing. Andy continues watching.

The Tour Guide steps over the white line, cleans the broken eggs off the glass with a rag and some sort of cleaning product. She might hum along to the piano while she does this.

From the stairwell we hear the Guard beat the person with the butt of his rifle. We hear the assailant crying out, pleading for his/her life. We hear the door to the street open and close, then silence.

The Guard returns to his post, wielding his weapon at port arms, his nostrils flaring.)

GUARD: Anyone else?

(The Tour Guide finishes cleaning, steps away from the glass, exits.)

After hours.

Lloyd is sitting very near the glass. He sits Indian-style, his IV rack wheeled beside him. He breathes on the glass, writes little things in the steam of his breath.

The Guard is removing his torso armor, wiping down his weapon.

LLOYD: Hey.

(The Guard doesn't respond.)

Hey.

(Lloyd taps on the glass.)

Come on, use your toy, talk to me.

(The Guard reluctantly engages the device, like a walkie-talkie, and uses it whenever he speaks to Lloyd.)

GUARD: What.

LLOYD: Don't you ever sleep?

GUARD: Not really.

LLOYD: Insomnia?

GUARD: Nope.

LLOYD: Bad dreams?

(The Guard says nothing, continues going about his business.)

I know: you're actually bionic. You have titanium femurs and digital corneas.

GUARD: I'll sleep when I die.

LLOYD: Do you take drugs to stay awake?

GUARD: Curious motherfucker, ain't you?

LLOYD: Where are you?

(The Guard doesn't answer.)

Come on, this isn't fair. You can see me.

GUARD: I'm on the other side of the glass.

(Beat.)

LLOYD: How long were you Special Ops?

GUARD: How'd you know I was Special Ops?

LLOYD: The Director told me . . . Did you kill a lot of people?

GUARD: Enough to make it worth my while.

LLOYD: Women and children?

(The Guard doesn't answer, continues wiping down his weapon.)

Screaming Middle Eastern babies with eyes like paper cuts?

(Again, the Guard doesn't answer.)

How tall are you?

GUARD: Why?

LLOYD: Just curious. Are you big?

GUARD: Big enough.

LLOYD: Where are you from?

GUARD: The United States of America . . . Detroit.

LLOYD: Do you ever look at me?

GUARD: No.

LLOYD: Why not?

GUARD: Because it's not my job to look at you. My job is to look
at them. To make sure nobody crosses the white line.

LLOYD: But they all went home.

GUARD: So now I don't gotta look at nobody.

LLOYD: Look at me.

GUARD: Fuck you.

LLOYD: I'm right behind you. Come on, Robocop.

GUARD: You a faggot or something? You got your dick all hard?

LLOYD: No.

GUARD: I don't feel like lookin' at your crazy ass.

(Beat.)

LLOYD: What if someone did rush the glass? What would you do?

GUARD: I'd kill the motherfucker.

LLOYD: You like killing people?

GUARD: Do you?

*(Lloyd says nothing. The Guard finally turns to him, studies
Lloyd for a moment. Then:)*

You tell people you weren't really part of the freak show
in Afghanistan; that you were just on a cleanup detail. But
I think you killed some people.

LLOYD: What makes you so sure?

GUARD: I can just tell.

LLOYD: By my savage, homicidal gait?

GUARD: Your eyes.

(Beat.)

LLOYD: You were over there, too?
GUARD: Hell yes I was over there.
LLOYD: Kabul?
GUARD: Kandahar.
LLOYD: How long?
GUARD: Long enough.

(Beat.)

LLOYD: You married?
GUARD: Yep.
LLOYD: Kids?
GUARD: I got a little girl.
LLOYD: How old?
GUARD: She'll be four next week.
LLOYD: What's her name?
GUARD: Jasmine.
LLOYD: Pretty name . . . Would you ever bring Jasmine here?
GUARD: To this place? Hell no. No kid should see this shit.

(Beat.)

LLOYD: What's your name?
GUARD: You know my name.
LLOYD: No I don't.
GUARD: It's Harris.
LLOYD: Your first name.
GUARD: Why?
LLOYD: Because I spend practically every waking hour of my life
     with you and I don't even know your name.
GUARD: . . . Darnell.
LLOYD: Why are you doing this job, Darnell?
GUARD: Because they pay me.
LLOYD: They pay you that well?

GUARD: I get benefits, retirement.

LLOYD: But you could do other things. You were fucking Special
    Ops. You could go into the Secret Service.

GUARD: The grass is always fuckin' greener.

(Pause.)

LLOYD: On my third week in Kabul we were going through the
    rubble of an apartment complex. This guy in my unit found
    a little girl alive, unscathed. Maybe eight years old. She was
    hiding in this little cinder-block bunker that had somehow
    survived the bombing. She was terrified. Her teeth were
    chattering. She was so hungry she had been trying to eat
    her headscarf . . .

GUARD: And then what?

(Lloyd says nothing.)

Y'all did some terrible shit to her, didn't you?

(Lloyd doesn't answer.)

You could've taken her out of there but you and your partner had yourselves a little joyful time?

(No answer.)

At least tell me that after you was through you put her out
of her misery.

(A silence. Then:)

LLOYD: I want to die, Darnell.

(Beat.)

GUARD: People who really want to die find a way, no matter what
. . . I saw a man pull his own eyes out. Portsmouth Naval
Prison. I was on suicide watch. First year they reopened
that fucking nightmare of a place. Motherfucker was seri-
ously suicidal so we took all his shit away from him. They
even shaved all his hair off—what little bit he had—'cause
they thought he would pull it out and try choking himself.
He was bare-assed naked in his cell. Bald. Shivering . . .
He wanted to die so bad he pulled his fucking eyes out . . .
You don't want it that bad.

*(Lloyd stands, wheels his IV stand back toward his bed.
He pulls his IV tubes out, then reaches into his pillowcase.
Removes a makeshift noose fashioned from a torn hospital
sheet.)*

What the fuck you doin'?

*(Lloyd approaches the showerhead, reaches up, tests its
weight-bearing possibilities. He then stands on a chair, loops
the makeshift noose over the shower nozzle, places the larger
portion over his head, kicks the chair out from under him
and proceeds to hang himself.)*

Lloyd!!! Lloyd what the fuck!!!

(The Guard starts pounding on the glass.)

Nurse!!! Nurse!!!

(He keeps pounding on the glass.)

NURSE!!!

*(An alarm sounds.
    Blackout.)*

PART TWO

Forty-eight hours later.

Lloyd has been secured to his mattress with heavy canvas straps that are bolted into the floor. There is also a cervical collar around his neck.

The flowers are still on the piano, though starting to wilt.

The Guard is at his post, staring daggers into the audience.

Lloyd is sleeping. After a long moment:

A new nurse, Joan, is seated on the piano bench, reading a magazine. She is attractive, mid-thirties.

Lloyd wakes up screaming, then regains his poise, clocks the new nurse. Then:

LLOYD: Who are you?

JOAN: I'm Joan.

LLOYD: Joan who?

JOAN: Joan your new nurse.

LLOYD: What happened to Andy?

JOAN: He's still here.

LLOYD: Since when do I need another nurse?

JOAN: Since you tried hanging yourself. The museum can't lose their prized subject.

(Beat.)

The Director tells me you were one of four people who answered the ad. One man was blind. Another was in his seventies. It's not likely they'd find a compelling nonvaccinated replacement.

LLOYD: So you've been brought in to keep me alive.

JOAN: We gotta get you through the next insufferable affliction.

LLOYD: Do you give handjobs? Just kidding . . . Will you unstrap me?

JOAN: Unfortunately I'm under strict orders.

LLOYD: I'm not in the mood to kill myself right now. Suicide's a mood thing, you should know that.

JOAN: Sorry.

(Lloyd smells something again.)

LLOYD: By the way, do you smell that?

JOAN: Smell what?

LLOYD: I think something's rotting. Something in the wall.

JOAN: I don't smell anything.

(Beat.)

LLOYD: So what's next on the docket, anyway, *Joan?*

JOAN: Cholera. The pulse just arrived while I was signing in. Enough of a dose to back up half the toilets in Manhattan.

LLOYD: Are you injecting me?

JOAN: Your friend Andy will have the privilege.

LLOYD: You must be pretty special for the museum to go after you.

JOAN: Let's just say I'm thorough.

LLOYD: Where are you from?

JOAN: A psych ward in Weehawken, New Jersey. There's an elderly patient there who has been living with a drug-resistant strain of Tuberculosis for over sixty years. Somehow he slipped through the cracks during the Great Vaccination. He's an incontinent schizophrenic who calls himself George Washingmachine. I was his sole caretaker for the past sixteen months.

LLOYD: So your reputation precedes you. Stick her with the wackjob who plays with his feces.

JOAN: You play with your feces?

LLOYD: Only after Beef Burgundy Tuesdays.

(Beat.)

About the hanging: I was just testing Andy.

JOAN: It took him a full cycle of CPR to revive you.

LLOYD: *That's* where the Dentyne Winter Ice came from!

(Joan crosses to his bedside, picks up his notebook off the floor, writes something down, holds it in front of him so he can read it. He looks at her. She nods. This is a very intense transaction and should take a moment to land. She then tears the piece of paper out of his notebook, folds it into fours and eats it. The rest of their encounter is a cover for what has been written down.)

So now you'll be around?

JOAN: Twenty-four-seven. Better get used to it . . . They tell me your recovery from the Black Death was nothing less than miraculous. You have quite the constitution.

LLOYD: I'm actually half catfish. You should see my insides . . . *(Referring back to what she wrote in the notebook)* You'll really do that?

(Andy enters with a hermetically sealed, armored silver box and a digital clipboard.
Joan closes the notebook.
Andy nods to Joan and Joan starts to undo the straps, freeing Lloyd.

Andy offers Lloyd the digital clipboard. Joan produces a digital pen. Lloyd uses the digital pen to sign something on the digital clipboard, then hands the clipboard and pen to Andy. Andy also signs the digital clipboard.

Andy then opens the silver box, producing the hypo. Joan produces an alcohol swab, cleans his arm. Andy kneels down, injects Lloyd with the hypo.)

Twenty-four hours later.
The Tour Guide appears on the audience side of the glass, just on the audience side of the white line. She is wearing a medical mask. She removes it, begins speaking.

TOUR GUIDE: Cholera is a severe bacterial infection that ravishes the intestines. The main symptoms include profuse watery diarrhea and vomiting. Transmission is achieved primarily by the acquisition of the pathogen through contaminated drinking water or infected food. The severity of the diarrhea and associated vomiting can lead to rapid dehydration and electrolyte imbalance, which can, in turn, lead to death. As recent as twenty years ago, cholera was a major cause of death in the world.

   Lights.

   Note the nurse's proximity to the subject's body, keeping him upright, literally touching his flesh. Note the committed physical effort.

Cholera was the subject of numerous great works of literature, including Albert Camus' *The Plague* and *Love in the Time of Cholera* by Gabriel García Márquez.

The great British author Rudyard Kipling wrote this poem:

Cholera Camp

We've got the cholerer in camp—it's worse than forty
    fights;
We're dyin' in the wilderness the same as Isrulites;
It's before us, an' be'ind us, an' we cannot get away,
An' the doctor's just reported we've ten more to-day!

    Oh, strike your camp an' go, the bugle's callin',
      The Rains are fallin'—
    The dead are bushed an' stoned to keep 'em safe
      below;
    The Band's a-doin' all she knows to cheer us;
    The chaplain's gone and prayed to Gawd to 'ear us—
      To 'ear us—
    O Lord, for it's a-killin' of us so!

Since August, when it started, it's been stickin' to our
    tail,
Though they've 'ad us out by marches an' they've 'ad us
    back by rail;
But it runs as fast as troop-trains, and we cannot get away;
An' the sick-list to the Colonel makes ten more to-day.

There ain't no fun in women nor there ain't no bite to
    drink;
It's much too wet for shootin', we can only march and
    think;
An' at evenin', down the *nullahs*, we can 'ear the
    jackals say,
"Get up, you rotten beggars, you've ten more to-day!"

'Twould make a monkey cough to see our way o' doin'
    things—
Lieutenants takin' companies an' captains takin' wings,
An' Lances actin' Sergeants—eight file to obey—
For we've lots o' quick promotion on ten deaths a day!

Our Colonel's white an' twitterly—'e gets no sleep nor
    food,
But mucks about in 'orspital where nothing does no good.
'E sends us 'eaps o' comforts, all bought from 'is pay—
But there aren't much comfort 'andy on ten deaths a day.

Our Chaplain's got a banjo, an' a skinny mule 'e rides,
An' the stuff 'e says an' sings us, Lord, it makes us split
    our sides!
With 'is black coat-tails a-bobbin' to *Ta-ra-ra Boom-
der-ay*!
'E's the proper kind o' *padre* for ten deaths a day.

An' Father Victor 'elps 'im with our Roman
    Catholicks—
He knows an 'eap of Irish songs an' rummy conjurin'
    tricks;
An' the two they works together when it comes to play
    or pray;
So we keep the ball a-rollin' on ten deaths a day.

We've got the cholerer in camp—we've got it 'ot an' sweet;
It ain't no Christmas dinner, but it's 'elped an' we must
    eat.
We've gone beyond the funkin', 'cause we've found it
    doesn't pay,
An' we're rockin' round the Districk on ten deaths a day!

    Then strike your camp an' go, the Rains are fallin',
      The Bugle's callin'!

The dead are bushed an' stoned to keep 'em safe
     below!
An' them that do not like it they can lump it,
An' them that cannot stand it they can jump it;
We've got to die somewhere—some way—
     some'ow—
We might as well begin to do it now!
Then, Number One, let down the tent-pole slow,
Knock out the pegs an' 'old the corners—so!
Fold in the flies, furl up the ropes, an' stow!
Oh, strike—oh, strike your camp an' go!
     (Gawd 'elp us!)

*(The red lights suddenly begin swirling. The Tour Guide
simply watches what's going on behind the glass. Andy and
Joan don masks, gloves, cover their exposed flesh.*

*Lloyd scurries to the toilet, clutching his sides, crying out,
shitting out his insides.*

*Andy stands beside Lloyd. Andy is doing everything in
his power to keep Lloyd upright and on the toilet while Joan
looks on.*

*Lloyd jumps off the toilet, pushing away from Andy. He
scurries into the corner, hugging his knees into his chest,
rocking back and forth. Eventually he passes out from
exhaustion. Andy and Joan carry Lloyd back to bed, strap
him down as the red lights continue.)*

Seventy-two hours later.

The red lights are off. Lloyd is no longer contagious, getting back to strength, still strapped into his bed. He has a visitor, his brother, Joe.

JOE *(Referring to the digs)*: So this is . . .

LLOYD: Fucking awesome?

JOE: It's like you're trapped in a science fiction novel.

LLOYD: I'm actually not trapped at all. I'm here by my own volition and I can leave anytime I want. Except when I'm septic. When I'm septic I'm on lockdown.

JOE: No shit. Wanna go get a burger? Just kidding.

(Beat.)

They told me what you tried to do to yourself, Lloyd.

(Lloyd says nothing. After an uncomfortable pause, Joe, starts walking around, taking in the various medical accoutrements.)

When does the next tour start?

LLOYD: Oh, they're out there right now.

(Joe crosses to the glass, puts his hand up to it, peers out.)

JOE: I don't see anything.

LLOYD: It's a special one-sided glass. They're out there twenty-one hours a day. The museum only closes between four and seven A.M.

JOE: Can they hear us?

LLOYD: Loud and clear.

JOE: It's like we're at the zoo.

LLOYD: You mean *they're* at the zoo. They paid money for a ticket. The simile only holds if we're the animals. Or I should say I'm the animal. You're just the animal's . . .

JOE: Human brother?

LLOYD: Exactly.

JOE *(Taking in the glass, perhaps touching it)*: One-sided glass, huh?

LLOYD: The museum believes it makes it easier for me to act naturally. If I could see them out there I might change my behavior.

JOE: So you . . . *(Gestures to the toilet, the shower)*

LLOYD: Yeah, I shit, shower, shave, jerk off . . . Not to mention scream, freak out, slip and fall in my own bodily fluids, and wallow in self-pity.

JOE: All for the amusement of others.

LLOYD: Amusement? This is ethnography, bro.

JOE: Ethnography?

LLOYD: Cultural anthropology. This is big word type shit.

(Joe backs away from the glass.)

JOE: I have to say you look pretty bad.

(Joe simply glances over at the toilet, looks away from it.)

LLOYD: How's Phoenix? Gotten any of the nuclear winter yet?

JOE: Not yet. So far the prevailing winds have been agreeable.

LLOYD: So while what's left of California smolders in its own post-holocaust ash, life goes on per usual in Phoenix.

JOE: I s'pose it does, yeah.

LLOYD: You ever feel weird about that?

JOE: I don't actually, no.

(Awkward pause.)

LLOYD: Yeah, you look amazing. Like you could take on a tiger shark. What are you benching these days?

JOE: Two-forty-five. We just had a new fitness center put in next to the—

LLOYD: That's fucking awesome. I can only do this for about five more minutes, Joe.

JOE: Do what?

LLOYD: This.

JOE: You asked.

LLOYD: What is it exactly that you want?

JOE: I was just hoping to talk to you.

(Beat.)

You know you're making national news. There are photographers downstairs. There's a whole media circus.

LLOYD: They're waiting for me to walk: VOLUNTEER DISEASE FREAK STEPS BACK INTO A PERFECT WORLD. What a news story . . . Could be bad for business.

JOE: That's a risk I'm willing to take.

LLOYD: What is it that you do again? Don't you own a bunch of hot dog stands or something?

JOE: Yeah, I do have all those hot dog stands. I also have that pharmaceutical company.

LLOYD: One doesn't "have" a pharmaceutical company, one actually "owns" one of those. One "has" hemorrhoids or anal warts.

JOE: Okay, I *own* a pharmaceutical company.

LLOYD: Yeah, what's that new drug you sell that makes people forget they're going to die—what's that called again?

JOE: Wellspring. And it doesn't make you forget you're going to die, it just makes you feel better.

LLOYD: But doesn't it block some receptor?

JOE: It doesn't block it, it—

LLOYD: *Tweaks* it?

JOE: It's like a vitamin. *(He produces a Wellspring sample)* Here's a sample, if you'd like to try it.

(Joe sets the sample of Wellspring on the piano, next to the vase of flowers.)

LLOYD: We can trick ourselves into thinking we're not going to die but it doesn't hide the fact that we're just monkeys with shit for brains.

JOE: I happen to think the human race is evolving.

LLOYD: Why, because we figured out how to kill some germs? Because now boys in the third grade have six-pack abs and some nine-year-old girl in Kenosha just ran a sub-five-minute mile? It still doesn't fix the fact that we come out of the womb pre-programmed to consume the shit out of everything in sight.

JOE: Look, I didn't come here to argue with you, Lloyd. Can we talk about something else?

LLOYD: Sure . . . So how's the homestead? The family flourishing?

JOE: Carla's great. The kids are growing like weeds. You should see Davey. The way he can throw a baseball. Six years old and he can throw it all the way to home plate from second base on a rope. And Katie's just as cute as can be.

LLOYD: How old is she again?

JOE: Katie's four. Four and a half next week . . . They're always asking about their Uncle Lloyd. They see pictures of you on the news. They get confused. Carla tells them you're doing this for the greater good.

LLOYD: I'm not.

JOE: . . . Then why are you doing it?

LLOYD: I don't know. I guess I fit the job description.

JOE: You could have a normal life, Lloyd.

LLOYD: You think so?

JOE: I know so. You could have anything you want.

LLOYD: You know, last time I visited you at your palatial home in Phoenix I walked into your bedroom while you were fucking Carla. I don't know why. I think I was hoping to borrow one of your seven-hundred-dollar T-shirts. I really wanted to know what it was like to feel such a high-quality threadcount against my nipples . . .

You were on top of Carla, really going at it. We made eye contact—Carla and me . . . When you came she made a face like she was swallowing crushed glass. You made a noise like a woman. Like you were being chased through a forest by a man with an ax. Then you collapsed on her and wept. Carla held you, stroked the back of your head . . . Carla and I never broke eye contact . . . While you wept all over your wife's tits like a child with a broken toy, she and I looked into each other's souls with such intensity I could feel my heart swell.

After that I went into one of your seven bathrooms— the one off the wing with the Japanese rock garden—and jerked off into a wad of scented Kleenex. And then I fed it to your dog.

A week later I left for Afghanistan.

(A long pause.
Joe turns to the piano, touches its surface.)

JOE: Your flowers are dying . . . How 'bout I take you out of here, Lloyd?

LLOYD: Oh, Joseph.

JOE: Put you on the Gulf Stream with me. You could stay with us in Phoenix until you get back on your feet. Carla's fixing up one of the guest rooms as we speak. Mom's coming to visit us next week.

LLOYD: Mom. Jesus. How is old horseface? She still in Leavenworth?

JOE: She's still in Leavenworth. Still sings in the church choir. Visits Dad's grave every Saturday. Waits for her magnolia tree to flower every spring . . . She can't even talk about what's going on. She thinks you're tinkering with God's plan. I think it would be good for us all to see each other again.

LLOYD: You gonna smuggle me into a cab? Stuff me under your arm like a football?

JOE: You said you could walk out of here anytime you wanted.

LLOYD: But imagine what all those reporters would say. Your association with me couldn't possibly be good for Wellspring. It would be a scandal.

JOE: Like I said: That's a risk I'm willing to take.

LLOYD: But why would you want me to return to my life of walking around shopping malls and eating everyone's caramel corn?

JOE: You could teach again.

LLOYD: I'm content. Let me be content.

JOE: But what the heck do you do all day?

LLOYD: What do you mean, what do I do? I get to lie around and be cared for. I'm like a really expressive houseplant.

JOE: Not my idea of a useful life, Lloyd.

LLOYD: Not all lives are useful ones, Joseph.

JOE: The shame is that you're squandering yours. And you're making a fool of yourself . . .

(Pause.)

You know you tell me that story about watching me and Carla make love and all the other stuff . . . Carla really cares about you Lloyd. She thinks you're smart. She thinks that underneath all your cynicism you have a good heart. People out there really, really care for you.

LLOYD: Hey, will you do me a favor?

JOE: Of course.

LLOYD: Come here.

(Joe approaches Lloyd.)

Closer.

(Joe bends down. Lloyd whispers something into his ear. Joe pulls away sharply, simply stares at his brother, stunned, confused.)

I won't even struggle. I'm told it only takes like twelve pounds of pressure. It'll look like you're comforting me. You can do it, Joseph.

(Joe doesn't move.)

Just pretend you're helping me sleep . . . Think about the pillow. How soft it is. *(Sincere)* Please?

(Joe simply stares at him, then presses the intercom.)

JOE: Nurse?

(Andy enters.)

I'd like to leave now.

LLOYD *(To Joe)*: No worries. I have other options. Give my best to Carla and Davey and Khaki.

JOE: It's Katie.

ANDY: The exit's this way.

(Joe starts for the exit, stops.)

JOE *(To Andy)*: Watch him closely.

ANDY: That's what they pay me for.

(Joe exits.
The Tour Guide enters holding a posted bill of some size,
turns to the glass.)

TOUR GUIDE: Lights.

(On the other side of the glass, the lights bump down so that
the audience can only see their reflection.)

This was just removed from the entrance to the museum . . .

(Reading from the posted bill:)

> The human animal is not a machine.
> The human animal is not made up of pulleys and
>   sprockets.
> The human animal is a womb-sprung organism meant to
>   pass through a natural life cycle.
> To live out its years biologically.
> To struggle with the world on its own terms.
> To confront failure.
> To grapple with its own imperfect corpus so that it may
>   not only fully know pain and suffering, but also its
>   converse: joy.
> The human animal evolved from the fish and the ape and
>   the seabird.
> The human animal is no more worthy of the earth than
>   the field mouse or the salamander.
> Our movement will do everything in our power to restore
>   a dignified, holistic legacy to the human race.
> Our movement will achieve our goal at all costs.
> Signed, Superwolf.

(She folds the poster into fours.)

(To the Guard) Mr. Harris, what do you have to say about
this Superwolf business?

GUARD: I say I never seen no wolf outdo no automatic weapon
before. Never seen that in my life.

TOUR GUIDE *(To the audience)*: We at the museum believe that it
is essential to know disease in an educative way. We believe
in the evolution of our species. We believe in technology
and medical improvement. *(To an audience member)* Aren't
you glad that you may have another fifty or sixty years to
live? *(To another audience member)* Don't you see quality
of life as an exciting commodity during this era of medical
and technological progress? *(To another audience member)*
Do you not still feel joy? I certainly do. I feel joy every
day of my life. I'm feeling joy right now as I'm looking at
all of you. And I look forward to living to be a hundred. I'm
sixty-two years old and don't I look fantastic? I don't look
a day over thirty, wouldn't you agree, sir? . . . So if there
are any of you Superwolves out there, beware. Right, Mr.
Harris?

(The Guard nods.)

Do indeed beware . . . *(She turns to the glass)* Lights?

*(The lights on the other side of the glass bump back up, the
audience reflection goes away, and Lloyd's world is again
revealed.*

*Lloyd has eaten all the Wellspring pills. He is dancing
to some crazy waltz music that is loudly piping in to the
audience. He frolics, jumps for joy, happier than he's ever
been in his life. He leaps across his room, grabbing invisible
rainbows, embracing elves and fairies. He tears his garment
off and celebrates his nudity, still waltzing.*

*Joan enters. He takes her and waltzes with her, and after
a few turns, it starts to get very dangerous and the music
grows very loud.*

Andy enters. While he attempts to overtake Lloyd and stop the dancing, the red curtain is drawn closed.

The music then ends abruptly.

There is a long pause and the audience should be very uncomfortable.

Muzak.

Just as the audience starts to fidget and behave as if it's an intermission, the curtain is opened.)

PART THREE

Seventy-two hours later.

Lloyd is sitting on his mattress, no longer strapped in, still recovering. Andy is seated on the floor beside him, reading Dr. Seuss's Green Eggs and Ham. *Andy's interest starts out as passive, but builds to intent listening, mild amusement, and at the end he is rapt.*

Andy closes the book. They sit in silence for a moment. Then:

ANDY: Wow.

LLOYD: I know, right?

ANDY: I've never read that out loud like that.

LLOYD: It starts to work on you.

ANDY: It really does.

LLOYD: If you're open to it.

ANDY: I felt like I was.

LLOYD: I felt you were, too.

ANDY: It's so . . . there's so much surrender in it.

LLOYD: Perhaps the single most underrated piece of twentieth-century literature. Everyone wants to talk about Pynchon and Updike and DeLillo. *Green Eggs and Ham* trumps all

of it. And with so few words! Theodor Seuss Geisel. So misunderstood.

(Beat. Andy watches Lloyd for a long moment.)

What?

ANDY: I think I want to kiss you.

LLOYD: Really?

ANDY: Should I not have said that?

LLOYD: It could be risky.

ANDY: Emotionally or health-wise?

LLOYD: What do you think?

ANDY: Well, your blood work came back negative. Your system
of recovery is sort of incredible . . . Can I?

LLOYD: Can you . . .

ANDY: Kiss . . . you?

LLOYD: Andy . . .

ANDY: No, you're right.

(A brief silence.)

I knitted you a scarf.

(He produces the scarf.)

LLOYD: You did. You did knit me a scarf.

ANDY: It's cashmere.

(Andy drapes the scarf around Lloyd's neck.)

LLOYD: Thanks, Andy.

ANDY: The color matches your eyes . . . Sometimes when I'm taking my break in the nurses' lounge, I . . .

LLOYD: You knit?

ANDY: I think about what it would be like to . . . *(Suddenly real-
izing the potential danger of Lloyd possessing a scarf)* Oh
Jesus, you can't have that!

(Andy takes the scarf back. An awkward pause. Then:)

I think you're a beautiful person, Lloyd. Out of all the things you could be doing with your life, you chose this.

LLOYD: I'm a creature in a cage. People are getting off watching me suffer.

ANDY: They're inspired by watching you recover. And by your willingness to be cared for. Being cared for is a lost art, Lloyd. No one knows what that means anymore. Caring *for* someone is easy, but *being cared for* . . . *allowing someone in* . . . I'll bet your mouth tastes like a tangelo.

(A brief, tense pause.
    Andy hesitates, then leans in, kisses Lloyd. They kiss for a long moment. The kiss ends.)

LLOYD: Does it?

ANDY *(Dazed)*: What?

LLOYD: Taste like a tangelo?

ANDY *(Almost in tears)*: Yes.

(Andy starts to breathe very intensely, not taking his eyes off of Lloyd.)

I hope we get to spend a hundred diseases together.

(Lloyd nods obliquely. Then:)

LLOYD: Andy?

ANDY: Yes, Lloyd?

LLOYD: I think I need to um . . .

ANDY: Oh, of course. You need help getting up?

LLOYD: I'd better use the bedpan. I'm still feeling pretty weak.

(Andy gives Lloyd his bedpan.)

ANDY: I'll be back for that.

LLOYD: Thanks, Andy.

(Andy exits. Lloyd considers the bedpan.
While Lloyd uses the bedpan, the Tour Guide enters, hold-
ing a letter-sized envelope. She removes a piece of paper,
unfolds it, speaks to the audience:)

TOUR GUIDE: The following is a document written by Dorothea
Dix to lay out the requirements for women who would work
in the nursing service for the Union Army during the American Civil War.

Circular No. 8.
By Dorothea Dix
Washington, D.C.
July 14, 1862.

No candidate for service in the Women's Department
for nursing in the Military Hospitals of the United
States will be received below the age of thirty-five
years, nor above fifty. Only women of strong health,
not subjects of chronic disease, nor liable to sudden
illnesses, need apply. The duties of the station make
large and continued demands on strength.

Matronly persons of experience, good conduct,
or superior education and serious disposition, will
always have preference; habits of neatness, order,
sobriety and industry, are prerequisites.

All applicants must present certificates of qualifi-
cation and good character from at least two persons of
trust, testifying to morality, integrity, seriousness and
capacity for care of the sick—

(A young woman, Erin, enters the theater, looks around,
confused. She is frighteningly shy.)

Hello.

ERIN: Hello.

TOUR GUIDE: Are you here for the presentation?

ERIN: Yes.

TOUR GUIDE: Did you purchase a ticket?

ERIN: Yes. They sent me up . . . they said there was a seat.

TOUR GUIDE: You're going to have to speak up, honey, I can't hear you.

ERIN *(Slightly louder)*: They said there was a seat.

TOUR GUIDE: Well, there's an open seat right over there.

(On the other side of the glass, Lloyd finishes with the bedpan and moves toward the piano.)

ERIN: Lloyd? *(To the Tour Guide)* Is that Lloyd?

TOUR GUIDE: That's Lloyd, yes.

ERIN: What's he doing?

TOUR GUIDE: Do you realize where you are, miss?

ERIN: Why is he behind that glass? *(Louder)* Lloyd!

TOUR GUIDE: He can't hear you, miss.

ERIN: Lloyd, it's Erin!

TOUR GUIDE: Miss—

ERIN: Why isn't he responding?

TOUR GUIDE: Because he can't hear you. He can't hear or see you.

ERIN: Why not?

TOUR GUIDE: Because that's the way it's set up.

ERIN *(Looking at the audience)*: Who are all these people?

TOUR GUIDE: They're guests of the museum.

ERIN: Why is he trapped in there? Did he do something? What did he do?

(Lloyd considers the flowers. He picks a petal, eats it.
Erin starts to fall apart.)

(To the Tour Guide, referring to the audience) Can he see them?

TOUR GUIDE: He can't see any of us. Miss, you're holding up the—

ERIN: Can he *hear* them?

TOUR GUIDE: Miss, if you'd like to visit with Lloyd, you'll have to go speak with the woman at the box office.

(Erin crosses the line and starts pounding on the glass.)

ERIN: Lloyd!!! Lloyd!!! Lloyd, it's Erin!!!

(The Guard rushes Erin, seizes her and escorts her firmly to the box office area. She can be heard screaming, "Lloyd!!! Lloyd!!! Lloyd!!!")

TOUR GUIDE *(To the audience)*: Sorry about that . . . That's never actually happened before.

(The Guard returns to his post, his weapon at port arms. He nods to the Tour Guide. She puts the envelope away, abandoning the letter.
On the other side of the glass, Lloyd starts to play the piano. Joan enters, watches him, undetected. After a moment, Lloyd senses her, stops playing.)

JOAN: Was that Debussy?

LLOYD: Nine Inch Nails, actually.

JOAN: Sounded like Debussy's *La Mer*.

LLOYD: It's all the same to me.

JOAN: I'd respectfully disagree. Debussy's descending minor chord arrangements are pretty unmistakably his own. How long have you played piano?

LLOYD: Since I was like four. It seems to be one of those instruments that can get you to play it no matter how much hatred you've developed for it over the years. I can't believe my hands even remember this shit.

JOAN: How does it make you feel to play it again?

LLOYD: How does it make me *feel* . . . Are you a shrink or a nurse?

JOAN: I'm a shrinking nurse . . . I'm serious.

LLOYD: It makes me feel like I'm fourteen. Like I can't do any-
    thing right.
JOAN: You play beautifully.
LLOYD *(Changing the subject)*: These flowers are dead.

(Joan crosses to the flowers, seizes the vase.)

Leave them.

(She leaves the flowers.)

Why did you come in here?
JOAN: Because I'm supposed to tell you that it's time for you to
    get sick again.
LLOYD: How much time do I have?
JOAN: Seventy-two hours . . . And you have a visitor.

*(She hands him a piece of paper. He reads it, folds it in half.
Lloyd watches her for a long moment.)*

What.
LLOYD: You smell nice.
JOAN: Thank you.
LLOYD: You always smell so nice . . . I've been having dreams
    about you.
JOAN: What kind of dreams?
LLOYD: A lot of them take place in this room. You mostly take my
    vitals. Sometimes you give me a sponge bath. I wake up and
    I can't tell if it really happened. Sometimes I wake with an
    ache . . . I'm a bag of rot. I disgust you.
JOAN: I think what you're doing is important.
LLOYD: And what about you?
JOAN: What about me?
LLOYD: Is what you're doing important?

(She doesn't answer.)

What exactly *are* you doing?

(She doesn't answer.)

We're all capable of terrible things. You know that, right?
JOAN: And we're also capable of greatness.
LLOYD: Do you think if you do something great that it cancels out
     something terrible?
JOAN: I guess that depends.
LLOYD: On how terrible the bad thing was?
JOAN: Or how great the good thing can be.

(Beat.)

LLOYD: That thing you wrote in my notebook . . . When?

(Andy enters. Lloyd moves away from the piano.)

ANDY: Your visitor.

*(Lloyd nods.
     Andy and Joan exit.
     Erin eases into the room.)*

ERIN: Hi, Lloyd.
LLOYD: Hey.
ERIN: I know this must be quite a . . .
LLOYD: Quite a what.
ERIN: A surprise.
LLOYD: It's okay. I get to approve all visitors.
ERIN: Well, thanks for approving me.
LLOYD: Sure.

(She watches him for a moment.)

ERIN: You look thin.
LLOYD: Well, I'm sort of constantly dying, so . . .

ERIN: Your hair.

LLOYD: They shave it.

ERIN: Oh, good. I thought . . .

LLOYD: It makes things easier.

ERIN: Are you in a lot of pain?

LLOYD: Not right now, no.

(Awkward pause.)

ERIN: Would you mind if I sat down?

LLOYD *(Referring to the piano bench)*: Not at all.

(She sits on the piano bench, he moves to the mattress. She looks around a bit, then watches Lloyd intently. She can barely keep it together.)

What.

ERIN: Lloyd . . .

LLOYD: Yes, Erin.

(She starts to cry.)

Erin, come on.

ERIN: This is just all so odd. Is there a private room?

LLOYD: For what?

ERIN: For talking.

LLOYD: No. No private room.

ERIN: Okay.

LLOYD: So if you need to say something to me, you should just say it.

(She goes into her purse, produces a small photograph, hands it to Lloyd. He looks at it for a long time.)

How old is he?

ERIN: Two. Almost two and a half.

LLOYD: What's his name?

ERIN: Benjamin. I call him Benji . . . He has your eyes.

LLOYD: I had no idea.

ERIN: After you left I tried tracking you down, but . . . It's been almost three years, Lloyd. Three years of nothing. And then I see all this stuff about you in the news . . . I thought you should know.

(Awkward pause.)

He's starting to get at that age.

LLOYD: What age is that?

ERIN: The age when they start to ask questions . . . He sleeps like you.

LLOYD: He often wakes up screaming?

ERIN: He makes the same face. Like he's listening to his favorite song . . . He called me a baked potato the other day.

(Beat.)

LLOYD: You still teaching?

ERIN: Uh-huh.

LLOYD: Third grade.

ERIN: Fourth and fifth. They moved me up.

LLOYD: Good for you.

ERIN: Yeah.

(Long pause.)

LLOYD: Tell him I died.

ERIN: Lloyd, please.

LLOYD: No, I'm serious.

ERIN: Died how?

LLOYD: Tell him I got mauled by wolves.

(Awkward pause.)

ERIN: Can I ask a question?

LLOYD: Ask away.

ERIN: Do you ever think about me?

LLOYD: Sure.

ERIN: Fondly?

(He doesn't answer.)

Because we had a lot of good times, Lloyd . . . It still doesn't make sense to me.

LLOYD: What doesn't make sense?

ERIN: The way you left.

LLOYD: Please don't do this, Erin.

ERIN: Lloyd, I've spent the last three years trying to put my life back together. You have no idea what I've been through. How hard it was to lose you and then bring a child into the world.

LLOYD: . . . I'm sorry.

ERIN: Don't you want to know your son?

(He says nothing.)

What am I supposed to say to him when he finds out who you are?

LLOYD: Tell him the truth.

ERIN: Which is what?

LLOYD: That I'm a coward.

ERIN: Is that what you really want?

LLOYD: Tell him I was a coward and I got mauled by wolves and I deserved it.

(Long pause.)

I'm not a good person, Erin.

ERIN: Yes you are.

(She starts to cry.)

You're just confused, Lloyd . . . You're confused.

LLOYD: Please leave.

(She regains her composure. She rises. He offers the picture.)

ERIN: Keep it. Our phone number's on the back, if you're ever
so moved.

(She bends down, kisses the crown of his head, then exits.
Lloyd stares at the photo. After a moment, he starts to
cry. It is savage grief. After a moment, he realizes that he's
being watched by the audience. He gets off the mattress,
approaches the glass, removes a piece of medical tape from
his IV port, tapes the photo of his son, face out, dead cen-
ter on the glass. A tense moment thickens. Then the Guard
breaks rank, crosses to the glass, places his body in front of
Lloyd's.)

TOUR GUIDE: Lights.

(The hospital light on the other side of the glass fades out, so
that the audience can only see their own reflection.
The Guard returns to his post.)

Four hours later.
  Hard lights snap on, on the other side of the glass.
  Lloyd is lying down on the floor, on his back.
  A Journalist mans a state-of-the-art recording device. He might speak with an Australian accent.

JOURNALIST *(Into the device)*: Testing, testing . . .

(The Journalist plays it back, hears his voice.)

There we go . . . Thanks for doing this, by the way . . . So first things first: Is it for humanity? Is it for fame?
LLOYD: I answered the ad. I interviewed. I passed the physical and here I am.
JOURNALIST: It was all that perfunctory. There was no ulterior motive.
LLOYD *(Ironic)*: You mean you didn't read the press release?
JOURNALIST: But surely you knew this would get attention.
LLOYD: It's a private museum. There aren't even a hundred seats out there. It's not like I get a cut of the box office.

JOURNALIST: I understand that, but the international interest—
LLOYD: Next question, please.

(The Journalist refers to his notes.)

JOURNALIST: Where were you when you answered the ad?
LLOYD: I was in a Pizza Hut in Aberdeen, Maryland.
JOURNALIST: He was eating pizza in a Pizza Hut. How wonderfully American.
LLOYD: I was actually stealing croutons from the salad bar.

(The Journalist makes a note in his notebook.)

The croutons told me to do it. That Pizza Hut in Aberdeen has incredibly talented, articulate croutons.
JOURNALIST: I'm told you weren't employed at the time.
LLOYD: I was basically just walking around.
JOURNALIST: Walking around where exactly?
LLOYD: At that time mostly the highways.
JOURNALIST: Walking around the highways doing what?
LLOYD: There are these old things called viaducts—these random highway bridges. Underneath them it's like time has stopped. It's a nowhere place.
JOURNALIST: What were you doing under these viaducts?
LLOYD: Camping. Getting out of the rain. Listening to the semis thundering overhead. I met a pervert named Cecil on 294, just south of Milwaukee. He was trying to get to this twelve-year-old boy named Clarke in Wauwatosa. We huddled together against the cold. I gave him a scarf and wished him luck.
JOURNALIST: You wished him luck on his journey toward little Clarke? You actually wished him luck?
LLOYD: Hey, I don't judge! Whatever gets us through the night, right?

(Beat.)

JOURNALIST: Do you have a particular cause in mind?

LLOYD: My mother was a nurse.

JOURNALIST: Is that true or are you just saying that?

LLOYD: It's true and I'm just saying that.

JOURNALIST: You realize you're the biggest story in this country since the bombing of California.

LLOYD: Who are you with again?

JOURNALIST: I work for myself. Why do you ask?

LLOYD: You seem a little green.

JOURNALIST: Trust me I'm fucking aces.

LLOYD: Is that a fake accent by the way? What's your name?

JOURNALIST: Hendricks Media Corp.

LLOYD: What's your first name?

JOURNALIST: Clive.

LLOYD: Clive Hendricks Media Corp. Imagine following that in homeroom.

JOURNALIST: I'd like to bring a TV crew in here.

LLOYD: Do you have a cigarette?

JOURNALIST: I was told this is a "no smoking" area.

GUARD *(Speaking into his walkie-talkie)*: NO SMOKING IN THE MUSEUM!

JOURNALIST *(Singsong, out)*: Not intending to, mate.

GUARD *(Into his walkie-talkie)*: ALL SMOKERS WILL BE ASKED TO LEAVE THE PREMISES IMMEDIATELY!

LLOYD: He'll fucking kill you, he's an animal.

(Beat.)

JOURNALIST: So the Black Death. What was that like?

LLOYD: It hurt a lot.

JOURNALIST: Go on.

LLOYD: I got ominous-looking welts on my neck. My teeth turned yellow. My tongue swelled. My armpits bled. I thought I was shitting my pants, but it was actually these things called buboes, which were ejaculating pus and blood from my groin area.

JOURNALIST: They told me they turned it back on the sixth day. They say one more day and you would have died.

LLOYD: They did indeed turn the fucker back, Clive Hendricks Media Corp. In front of a full house, while I was screaming in Farsi.

JOURNALIST: You speak Farsi?

LLOYD: No, I was just saying that.

JOURNALIST: And cholera?

LLOYD: Cholera . . . hmmm . . . I could write songs about cholera.

JOURNALIST *(Mildly amused)*: What's it like, going through all of this in front of an audience?

LLOYD: I'm just a polar bear. *(Referring to the audience)* Why don't you ask them?

(The Journalist turns toward the glass, considers the audience, then returns to the interview.)

JOURNALIST: And how are you feeling now?

LLOYD: Oh, I'm great. I'm pretty much high all the time.

JOURNALIST: What kind of pain relief are you currently on?

LLOYD: I think this is Dilaudid. *(Offering to remove his IV)* Care for a splash?

JOURNALIST: No thanks.

(Beat.)

Was there ever a moment when you regretted your choice to volunteer?

LLOYD: The moment they started saving me.

(The Journalist makes a note, presses on.)

JOURNALIST: And next is . . .

LLOYD: Blackfrost. I'm told I might go blind. I'll have to learn braille and start feeling people's faces.

JOURNALIST: And what do you do in the meantime?

LLOYD: In the meantime, they cleanse my system, fatten me up.

JOURNALIST: You're so fully exposed out here. Your shower has no curtain. Your toilet, no stall. I'm told the audience watches your boils get lanced.

LLOYD *(Imitating him)*: I'm told the audience watches your boils get lanced.

(The Journalist laughs. Then:)

JOURNALIST: Is there no sense at all that you're being exploited?

(Lloyd doesn't answer.)

I think this is a question currently on a lot of people's minds.

LLOYD: I just want to be loved, Clive.

(The Journalist is amused.)

JOURNALIST: How would you feel about my bringing a camera crew in here?

LLOYD: Could be dangerous. I could be septic. You never know what might start ejaculating from the welts on my side.

JOURNALIST: I'm told you won't be contagious for another sixty-eight hours.

LLOYD: You want to sell my sores to Bausch & Lomb? Johnson & Johnson?

JOURNALIST: Try Nike. Try the United States Army.

LLOYD: "Be All You Can Be." That's rich.

JOURNALIST: Well, you are a veteran. They see you as one of their finest. And hundreds of thousands see you as the martyr for your generation.

LLOYD: Martyr in what capacity exactly?

JOURNALIST: Well, I imagine there's a tremendous amount of national shame. After the bombing of California, the U.S. didn't exactly sit back and swallow its pride. You made half the Middle East disappear . . . And there's also the sheer boldness of defying the first generation of a super race. People are living to be a hundred and ten years old, and here you are taking on plagues.

(Lloyd is drawn to a space in the wall, between his mattress and the piano. He starts to sniff at it, on all fours.)

People are looking to you, mate. I bring a camera crew in here and you could make a huge difference.

LLOYD: How much of a cut do I get if I agree to let you film me?

JOURNALIST: The publicity would make your future. You'd have book deals. There'd be a bidding war for the movie rights. More fame than you could imagine. Do you have an agent? I'd be happy to recommend someone.

LLOYD: I want an amount in dollars.

(The Journalist turns off the recording device.)

Three percent? Four?

JOURNALIST: You're out of your fucking mind.

LLOYD: Hey, I got a kid, Clive Hendricks Media Corps! He's two and his name is Benji! *(He grabs the photo and shows it to the Journalist)* . . . I get four-and-a-half percent or you never step a foot near this place again.

(The Journalist stares at him. Lloyd seizes the Journalist's hand, pulls it under his hospital gown, presses it firmly to his abdomen.)

You feel that?

(The Journalist tries to pull his hand away.)

You feel the rot?

(The Journalist struggles, but Lloyd holds firm.)

You really think you can sell that?

(The Journalist manages to yank his hand away. He franti-cally presses the intercom.)

JOURNALIST: Nurse! Nurse!

(The Journalist dives for the toilet, vomits. Andy rushes in.)

(Breathing heavy, from the toilet) I need to sterilize my hand! . . . Immediately!

(Andy ushers the Journalist away. The Journalist runs back to retrieve the recording device, then rushes out.)

After hours.
   That same night.
   Joan's back is against the glass. She speaks to Lloyd.

JOAN: There are thirty-seven of us. We're a combination of nurses, former nurses, a few teachers, a firefighter, a civil liberties lawyer, a former emeritus Ivy League professor, a former Jesuit priest and several others. We're scattered around the United States and we meet twice a year and think tank and strategize ways to put our mission into action. We've all taken an oath. We've all been marked. We're all willing to die for the cause . . . If we fail our mission we all meet in Madison, Wisconsin, three Sundays from now and drink twelve ounces of a fast-acting solution that will end our lives in six minutes.

(Beat.)

LLOYD: Why Madison, Wisconsin?
JOAN: Centrally located.

LLOYD: How have you been marked?

(Joan pulls her hair up, bearing the nape of her neck. He studies it.)

GUARD *(Over the intercom)*: So what's your plan? You gonna get Lloyd to shit in a bag and go dump it in a water fountain?

(The Guard enters through the nurses' entrance. He is behind the glass now, wearing civilian clothes, carrying a gym bag.)

(To Lloyd) Lloyd, what do you get in return?

LLOYD: Your face.

GUARD: What about my face?

LLOYD: I like it.

GUARD *(To Joan)*: Nurse, I think you seriously misunderstand something. Lloyd don't wanna die. He wants to keep being saved. 'Cause he into suffering. 'Cause he feels real bad about some shit he did. Some seriously questionable shit he did, ain't that right Lloyd?

(Lloyd says nothing.
  Beat.)

I should turn your ass in, Nurse.

(She says nothing.)

I could kill you right now.

JOAN: Jasmine is part of the first generation of a super race.

GUARD: How the fuck you know I got a daughter?

JOAN: Do you really want her to not know suffering? Real suffering? Don't you want her to appreciate her health? To truly know what empathy is?

(No response.)

This system that you're protecting is corrupt, Darnell.

GUARD: Is it?

JOAN: It's synthetic, and it turned you into a killing machine. And it could do the same thing to Jasmine.

GUARD: Stop using her name.

JOAN: It's a beautiful name.

(Beat.)

GUARD: You think you special 'cause you an extremist. 'Cause you and your smart friends got bored and decided to cook up some half-baked ideology.

JOAN: What's the difference between my extremism and your extremism?

GUARD: The difference is I ain't no terrorist.

JOAN: What you did in Afghanistan wasn't terrorism?

GUARD: I was in service of the United States of America.

JOAN: But you were serving the most corrupt nation on the planet. Red Rover, Red Rover, send Harris right over.

GUARD: And what are you serving? God? The Easter Bunny?

JOAN: I don't believe in God.

GUARD: Then what?

JOAN: Something greater.

(A tense pause. Then:)

GUARD: So whatchu gonna do?

JOAN: The question is, what are you going to do, Darnell?

GUARD: I'm standing right here.

JOAN: So am I. *(Referring to Lloyd)* And so is he.

(The Guard looks at Lloyd and Joan for a long time.)

GUARD: What do you want, Lloyd?

LLOYD: Hey, I'm with the Easter Bunny.

GUARD: Fuck that. What do you want?

(A charged stillness thickens between the three of them. Then the Guard exits through the nurses' door.
　　Beat.)

JOAN: Are you with me?
LLOYD: Yes.

(Lloyd nods. Joan crosses to him, touches his face.)

PART FOUR

The following afternoon.

The Guard is at his post, wearing his torso armor, holding his weapon at port arms.

The Tour Guide appears in front of the audience. She orates the following while, on the other side of the glass, Andy and Joan prepare another injection. The same exact sign-off ritual on the digital clipboard is repeated here.

TOUR GUIDE: Blackfrost, or "The Bells," as it was also known, was a short-lived, but brutal, sexually transmitted pandemic that swept across the northeast United States fifteen years ago, in 2038, with symptoms including extreme fever, blackened urine and chills so unbearable that victims believed they were freezing to death. They often reported the sensation that ice was forming in their lungs. *(She finds someone in the audience)* You remember this, right? *(She finds somebody else)* How awful that was?

Lights.

Eventually, victims of this brutal bacterial infection would go blind and were wracked with such intense hysteria that they would invariably claim they could hear the sound of church bells.

After symptoms became manifest, one who contracted Blackfrost only lived for three days, sometimes four, and the death was brutally painful due to the toxin the bacteria unleashed. Blackfrost produced extremely graphic septic, intestinal hemorrhaging that would often burst through the skin. If you were within fifty feet of a death it was likely that you would become infected, so at the height of Blackfrost, it wasn't uncommon to see people suddenly breaking into desperate paranoid sprints.

Blackfrost was particularly prolific in urban areas. In New York City alone, Blackfrost took over one hundred and eighty thousand people before a cure was discovered at Columbia University's Center for Social Disease. However, thousands of lives were still lost because the antitoxin needed to be administered continuously until the victim recovered. Any interruption in treatment often proved fatal.

(Joan and Andy leave Lloyd on his mattress. He sleeps.

After a long moment, Lloyd sits up very quickly. The red lights start swirling. He mutters to himself. He rises and starts to walk circles, pacing around the room. He tries to sit at the piano, can't get comfortable, rises, continues walking, muttering to himself. He eats a dead flower. He starts to clutch his sides, waves away invisible insects. He screams. He falls onto his mattress, curls into a fetal position. He screams again, shivering, his teeth chattering. He attacks the glass three times. He passes out on his mattress and sleeps. The red lights continue to swirl.

While Lloyd sleeps, Joan enters, check his vitals, his meds, then simply sits at the foot of his mattress, watching Lloyd sleep.

Andy enters and sits at the piano, starts to play.

The Tour Guide sings a ballad, while Joan, simply watches Lloyd.

*Lloyd wakes and climbs up off his mattress. He moves over
to the wall and begins to dig. He removes a dead pigeon from
the wall, and carries it back to his mattress, laying it before
Joan. Joan caresses his face, his forehead.
The Tour Guide sings:)*

It's not in the things that you do
It's not in the words you can write
It's not in the books
It's not what they took
It's not in the fields where they fight

It's easy to sit on a stool
It's easy to find your way down
It's easy to fish
It's easy to wish
It's easy to laugh at a clown

And it's a long way down
It's a long way down
A long way down
For your pity

Remember the size of my hands
Remember the length of my bones
Remember my skin
Remember my sins
Remember my breath

It's only a few days away
It's only a few moments more
It's only the night
It's only the night
It's only a face at my door.

(Erin enters. Andy and Joan exit. It should be clear that we are experiencing Lloyd's dream now. Erin is pregnant and wearing a hospital garment. She stands over Lloyd, straddling him. Her water breaks on his chest.)

And it's a long way down
It's a long way down
A long way down
For your pity

And it's a long way down
It's a long way down
A long way down
For your pity.

(Blackout.
    Some time passes.)

Lights up.
   Ninety-six hours later.
   *Lloyd wakes. Joan is once again in the room. Lloyd is
wrapped in blankets, in the fetal position. Blackfrost is starting
to take hold.*

LLOYD: I heard s-s-singing. Were you s-s-singing?

   *(Joan doesn't answer, simply watches him for a moment.
Then:)*

Hey, what's your last name, anyway?

   (She doesn't answer.)

   I know Andy's last n-n-name.
JOAN: If Andy shared that information with you then that's
   Andy's prerogative.
LLOYD: I bet it's like Johnston. Or Stone. Joan Stone.
JOAN: Roll onto your side.

(He does so.)

LLOYD: Or Rodriguez. J-J-Joan Rodriguez.

(She produces an old mercury thermometer, takes his temperature the old-fashioned way.)

Oh, Nurse Joan. Naughty, naughty.

(Joan studies her watch, eventually removes the thermometer from his rectum.)

How's my f-f-fever?

JOAN: 103.4.

LLOYD: You're so pretty. That's such a fucking cliché. A pretty nurse. It's like a fat chef. Or a gay d-d-dance captain.

(Andy enters.)

Andy, Joan won't t-t-tell me her last name.

ANDY: Lloyd, if Joan doesn't want to share that information with you then that's Joan's prerogative.

(Andy wands Lloyd.)

Joan, I just recorded his temperature at 103.4, but five minutes ago you logged him at 99.9.

JOAN: I took it rectally.

LLOYD: *Esta muy fantastico.*

JOAN: Maybe something's wrong with the wand.

(Joan wipes Lloyd's brow, Andy looking on. Andy holds his hand out for the rag.)

ANDY *(To Joan):* It's time for your break.

(Joan hands Andy the rag, exits. Andy sits where she was sitting, resumes dabbing at Lloyd's forehead with the cool rag.)

I found a copy of *The Cat in the Hat*. Shall I bring it in?

(Lloyd nods.)

I was thinking about talking to the Director about bringing groups of children to the museum. Only at certain times, of course. We could call it "Reading Hour with Lloyd." They could watch me read to you. And watch you listen. This thing of reading to the ill—it was an important part of convalescence. It happened. Do you think you would be interested in that? . . . Imagine an audience filled with kids. I think that would be really beautiful.

LLOYD: But we wouldn't be able to see them.

ANDY: But just knowing they're out there.

(Andy continues wiping Lloyd's brow.)

LLOYD: Isn't *The Cat in the Hat* about ch-ch-chaos?

ANDY: But the children love him. *Bump!* . . . And there's Up, Up with the Fish . . . And Thing One and Thing Two, their kites . . .

LLOYD: "What would you do if your mother asked you?"

ANDY: What?

LLOYD: It's the last line of the b-b-book.

ANDY: Oh, of course.

LLOYD: It's basically about how chaos teaches us how to lie to our m-m-m-mothers.

ANDY: Or how we are easily seduced by anarchy . . . Are you easily seduced by anarchy, Lloyd.

(Lloyd doesn't answer. They stare at each other for a long moment.)

Think about that reading hour idea. I'll run it by the Director.

(Andy exits.)

After hours.

That same evening.

The red lights are off.

Lloyd is wedged in the corner, covered in blankets, shivering.

On the audience side of the glass, the Guard is removing his torso armor. He uses his walkie-talkie device to speak to Lloyd.

GUARD: The other day my little girl asked me what I do? I told her I looked after this man who gets sick in front of people. She said, "What's sick, Daddy?"

LLOYD: What'd you t-t-tell her?

GUARD: I told her it was like getting old too fast. She don't know what the motherfucking word means . . .

When I was a boy I had a cold once. I remember sneezing a lot. I fake sneezed for my daughter. Now she tries to fake sneeze all the time. She sounds like a little cuckoo clock. "I'm sick, Daddy," she says. "Save me, I'm sick." Then she sneezes. It's cute as hell, it really is . . .

She says she wants to meet you . . . She asked me your name. I told her you don't have one. I told her we just call you The Subject.

(The Guard produces a small snapshot from his wallet, presses it to the glass.)

That's her there, see?

LLOYD: It's one-sided g-g-glass, remember? . . . Describe her to me.

(The Guard looks at the snapshot.)

GUARD: She's tall for her age. Forty-three inches. Big brown eyes . . . She's pigeon-toed, takes after her father in that respect. She's got big feet and she can be clumsy, but she'll grow into them . . . Her smile makes you forget where you are. Her eyes light up when I walk into the room . . . Her voice is like music . . .

LLOYD: She sounds b-b-beautiful.

(Beat.)

GUARD: When I was in Kandahar we were on a recon mission and we came upon all these babies that had been left in the street. Abandoned fucking babies. Dozens of them, covered in ash, exposed. Our job was to retrieve the live ones, get them medevaced out. Most of them was cooked. But a few was still hanging on. They looked old. Faces shriveled. Hearts beating all fast. Barely anything behind their eyes . . . We could only save four of them. Four of about sixty . . . One of them died in my arms. Turned blue as paint right in my arms . . .

When I came back I was awarded the Distinguished Service Cross. I was up for a big promotion, but I opted out . . . I was over there before the bombing started. I killed hundreds of people. Maybe even a thousand. Never thought twice about it . . . But to have something like that go in your arms. Something as small as that . . .

(Joan enters.)

JOAN *(To Lloyd)*: He still out there?

(Lloyd nods. Joan moves to the glass, stands very close to it.)

(To the glass) Thank you.

(The Guard moves to the glass, stands very close to it, directly opposite Joan. He stands there for a long moment, and then exits with his gear.)

How are you feeling?

LLOYD: C-c-cold. My throat feels like it's closing and my piss is starting to resemble m-m-motor oil, but mostly I'm fucking f-f-freezing. *(Pause)* This group you belong to—

JOAN: It's not a group. It's a Movement. We're not a fucking rock band . . . After it's done, I'll take you wherever you want to go.

LLOYD: You mean Us.

JOAN: Of course. Us. I'll take us wherever you want to go.

LLOYD: B-b-because I want you with me. Promise me.

JOAN: I promise.

(She takes his hand, puts it down her pants. He feels her.)

LLOYD: Is that m-m-me making you wet, or the M-m-movement?

JOAN: You.

(She nods, breathes harder, swoons a bit, his hand still between her legs.)

How do you want it?

LLOYD: Under the shower. Under the w-w-warm water.

(She takes his hand, leads him to the shower, turns the water on, puts his hand under it.)

JOAN: That good?

LLOYD: Hotter.

(She adjusts the water.)

JOAN: How's that?

(He nods. He faces the shower nozzle, his back to the audience. Joan goes to her knees, lifts his hospital gown, takes him in her mouth. He almost falls from the pleasure. She has to keep him standing upright.)

LLOYD: I'm gonna c-c-come.

(She stops, lowers her pants and puts him in her. They fuck hard and fast. It is as intense as it is brief. After Lloyd orgasms, he is terribly weakened, falls to the floor.

Joan turns the water off, goes into her bag, removes a kit for taking blood: a rubber hose, a tourniquet, a syringe, etc. She takes his arm, finds a good vein and taps it, drawing blood into the bag. Lloyd, though considerably weakened, is conscious throughout. He can't take his eyes off her. The drawing of the blood may take some time. Joan gently sings to him, soothes him, caressing his head, his face. At some point Lloyd vomits something darker than blood.

After Joan completes the blood work, she helps Lloyd to bed. He is shivering horribly, starting to go blind. He mutters to himself indecipherably. He is sweating profusely, convulsing, whimpering. She covers him with a thick wool blanket.

Andy enters carrying a bag of fluid. He is wearing protective gear. Joan quickly covers her face with the mask.)

ANDY: Joan, can I speak with you for a moment?

(A tense pause.)

When I checked on Lloyd earlier I noticed that his bag of antitoxin was incorrectly filled.

JOAN: That bag you're holding there?

ANDY: Yes. This was the bag that was connected to him.

JOAN: Is it marked as the antitoxin?

ANDY: Yes, but that's not what's in this bag.

JOAN: What's in it?

ANDY: Normal saline.

JOAN: Normal saline.

ANDY: Yes, normal saline . . . Did you do that? Because I didn't.

JOAN: What are you suggesting, Andy?

ANDY: I'm not suggesting anything. If you made a mistake you should own up to it, that's all. Did you make a mistake?

JOAN: I honestly couldn't tell you.

ANDY: Lloyd's life is in our hands, Joan! Any interruption in his treatment puts him in tremendous peril!

JOAN: And how do you know that that's not the antitoxin?

ANDY: Because I sent it to the lab and had it tested.

JOAN: Oh.

ANDY: Yeah.

JOAN: So what you're telling me is that you're holding a bag of normal saline.

ANDY: A thousand milliliters of normal saline, yes.

JOAN: And the bag that is currently feeding his IV is the correct antitoxin.

ANDY: Yes.

JOAN: Good work, Andy.

ANDY: Why are you all wet?

JOAN: I'm all wet because there's water on me. What made you decide to take the bag to the lab?

ANDY: I noticed that his symptoms haven't been improving. He's been responding so well to the other treatment so I figured something was wrong.

JOAN: Did you switch it?

ANDY: Of course.

JOAN: And you're absolutely one hundred percent medically certain that he is currently on the antitoxin.

ANDY: I am absolutely one hundred percent medically certain, this is correct.

(Joan turns away from Andy, crosses to the IV rack, produces a small deadly knife, stabs a hole in the IV bag, then disengages Lloyd's IV.)

What are you doing?

(Andy charges toward Joan. She stabs him fiercely in the stomach. He falls to his knees. She cuts his throat ear-to-ear.
Joan puts her knife away, sits on the piano bench for a moment, breathes, gathers her will, produces a cell phone, dials, waits.)

JOAN *(Into phone)*: Hey, it's me . . . It's done . . . Five minutes. *(She hangs up)*

(She moves to Lloyd, attempts to get him out of bed any way possible, lifting him from under his shoulders, moving his legs, etc.)

Lloyd . . . Lloyd, it's time. We have to go.

LLOYD *(A mumble)*: I c-c-can't see . . . I c-c-can't see . . .

JOAN: We can do this, Lloyd! Come on!

(Lloyd falls to the floor. She pulls him up. He falls again. She manages to get him to his feet and out the door.
Andy is left bleeding to death on the floor.
The Tour Guide slowly draws the red curtain across the scene, staring at the audience.)

EPILOGUE

Joan speaks directly to the audience, no longer behind glass:

JOAN: So the driver was waiting for us on the corner of Delancey
and Orchard. He drove us to Penn Station, where Lloyd
and I took an overnight train to Chicago. In the sleeping car
I held him while he shivered and cried and complained of
the ice that was spidering in his lungs. When we arrived at
Union Station, I gave him a strong dose of Dilaudid and put
him in a Dunkin' Donuts while I delivered a small, refriger-
ated cooler containing 150 cc's of Lloyd's infected blood to
my contact on the corner of Clark and Van Buren. He would
pass it along to a lab technician at the University of Chicago who would transform it into a communicable microbe
that would be injected into a thousand heads of livestock
and scourge the largest post-fluorinated water supply in the
upper-Midwest.

After I went back and got Lloyd at the Dunkin' Donuts
we somehow made it to a car that was waiting for us on the
corner of LaSalle and Van Buren. Lloyd wanted to drive
down to Leavenworth, Kansas, so he could say good-bye to

his mother, but I was able to convince him that this wasn't a good idea because they would be waiting for us there. They, meaning the police. The FBI. So we called her from a truck stop just outside of Ames, Iowa. Somehow I imagined a small blue house with a shoveled driveway. A plastic Santa Claus illuminated in the front yard. Christmas lights twinkling from the eaves.

Lloyd's mother's voice was small and far away. She spoke with a faint Midwestern accent. I imagined her washing carrots in her kitchen sink. In a pink twinset and a full white skirt, something from a hundred years in the past. She told me she didn't have a son named Lloyd.

I put the phone to Lloyd's ear and he mouthed the words, "Mom . . . Mom," but no sound came out.

Like a guppy in an empty fishing pail.

I took the phone back. "Lloyd's going blind," I told her. "He's going to die and he wants to say good-bye."

"I only have one son," she said. "His name is Joseph and he lives in Phoenix, Arizona."

I imagined her hands trembling with rheumatism.

That night Lloyd and I slept in a motel on the western edge of Kansas and in the morning drove west, to the desert.

This was his final wish.

He wanted to feel the wrath of the sun beating down on him.

We arrived in the Mojave by sunset the following evening. I had been keeping him high, but the Dilaudid was running out and I knew I would later need some for myself.

Lloyd's urine had turned from brown to black and he kept saying he could hear the faint sound of church bells.

We pulled off of Highway 66 and found a small ghost town called Ludlow. We parked in front of a boarded-up café whose adobe walls had been scarred by the winds and sand. We walked very slowly out behind the café, perhaps two hundred yards or so. The sky was rich with orange and purple light. The buzzards pinwheeled above us like slow black rags indifferently dropped from the hand of God. There was a long, smooth rock with a flat surface that could be comfortably lain upon.

This is where I left Lloyd to die. Walking away from him was the most difficult thing I've ever done because . . . well, because I *felt* for him.

I imagined the bells in his head.

Church bells drowning out the sound of the screeching birds.

I continued on alone to Los Angeles, my body ripe with disease, a small black spot already starting to form on the underside of my arm.

(She lifts her arm to show the spot.)

The devastation after the desert was indescribable.

Winter at the edge of the Mojave.

Ash.

I drove north to Utah and two days later found myself in the Uinta Mountains: the cleanest place I have ever seen in my life.

And now I am on top of a mountain, nine thousand feet above everything, looking out over a clear, glassy lake.

And you people are fishing and hiking and riding horses along the ridges.

As I descend to you, baring my spotted arms and dim teeth, as I hurl myself into your arms and give you this beautiful, perfect plague, will you still love me? *(Making direct eye contact with someone in the audience)* Will you? *(And eye contact with another)* Will you nurse me when I fall at your feet?

My tongue blackening.

The jellies of my eyes melting into the back of my throat.

(Lights fade to black.)

END

ADAM RAPP is an award-winning playwright, theater director, novelist and filmmaker. He is the author of numerous plays, which include *Nocturne* (American Repertory Theater, New York Theatre Workshop, Almeida Theatre in London, Traverse Theatre in Edinburgh), *Faster* (Rattlestick), *Animals and Plants* (A.R.T.), *Finer Noble Gases* (26th Humana Festival, Rattlestick, Edinburgh Fringe, Bush Theatre in London), *Stone Cold Dead Serious* (A.R.T., Edge Theatre), *Blackbird* (Bush Theatre, Edge Theatre), *Gompers* (Pittsburgh City Theatre, Arcola Theatre in London), *Essential Self-Defense* (Playwrights Horizons/Edge Theatre), *American Sligo* (Rattlestick), *Bingo with the Indians* (Flea Theater), *Kindness* (Playwrights Horizons), *The Metal Children* (Vineyard Theatre), *The Hallway Trilogy* (Rattlestick), *The Edge of Our Bodies* (36th Humana Festival, Guthrie Theater), *Dreams of Flying Dreams of Falling* (Atlantic Theater Company) and *Red Light Winter* (Steppenwolf, Scott Rudin Productions at Barrow Street Theatre), which won Chicago's Jeff Award for Best New Work, an Obie Award and was a finalist for the 2006 Pulitzer Prize. He has published eight novels for young adults, including *The Buffalo Tree* (Front Street Books), *Under the Wolf, Under the Dog* (Candlewick Press; finalist for the *L.A. Times* Book Prize), *Punkzilla* (Candlewick Press; 2010 Michael J. Printz Honor Book) and *The Children and the Wolves* (Candlewick Press; named one of the Best Books of 2012 by *Kirkus Reviews*). He is also the author of the adult novel *The Year of Endless Sorrows* (Farrar, Strauss & Giroux) and the graphic novel *Ball-Peen Hammer* (First Second Books), which he is currently developing as a series for HBO. As a filmmaker he wrote and directed the features *Winter Passing*, an Official Selection of the 2005 Toronto Film Festival, and *Blackbird*, which he adapted from his play. *Blackbird* was an Official Selection of South By Southwest and the Edinburgh International Film Festival, won Best Narrative Feature at the Charlotte Film Festival and earned Rapp a Special Jury Award for Achievement in Directing from the Florida Film Festival. Most recently, he directed the independent feature *Why Now?!* starring Marisa Tomei, Sam Rockwell and Brian Geraghty. As a theater director, he directed the world premiere of Karen O's psycho opera *Stop the Virgens* for The Creators Project at St. Ann's Warehouse, which was then selected for the Vivid Live Festival where it sold out the Sydney Opera House for six performances. Last fall, he directed the world premiere of his play *Through the Yellow Hour* Off-Broadway at Rattlestick. He also directed Sam Shepard's *True West* at Actors Theatre of Louisville, which went on to be named one of the 2012 Best Moments in Culture by Louisville's NPR affiliate, WFPL. His production of *Finer Noble Gases* garnered a Fringe First Award at the 2006 Edinburgh Fringe Festival, where he received *The List Magazine*'s Best Newcomer Prize. His playwriting honors include Boston's Elliot Norton Award, the Helen Merrill Award, the 2006 Princess Grace Statue, a Lucille Lortel Playwright's Fellowship and the Benjamin H. Danks Award from the American Academy of Arts and Letters. PEN recently honored him with the PEN/Laura Pels International Foundation for Theater Award.